LUTAH MARIA RIGGS

A Woman in Architecture

LUTAH MARIA RIGGS

A WOMAN IN ARCHITECTURE
1921 – 1980

DAVID GEBHARD

CAPRA PRESS

In cooperation with the

SANTA BARBARA MUSEUM OF ART

Printed in the United States of America.

Typesetting by Pagination Station.
Production Direction by Denise Eltinge.
Photography by Marvin Rand and Anthony Peres.
Illustrations from the University of California, Santa Barbara.

LIBRARY OF CONGRESS CATALOGING-IN-PUBLICATION DATA

Gebhard, David
Lutah Maria Riggs : a woman in California architecture, 1921-1980 /
by David Gebhard : photographs by Marvin Rand.
p. cm.

Includes bibliographical references and index.
ISBN 0-88496-352-7 (pbk.) : $20.00
1. Riggs, Lutah Maria, 1896- . 2. Architects--California--Biography.
3. Architecture, Modern--20th century--California.
I. Title
NA737.R54G4 1992
720'.92--dc20
[B] 92-15081
CIP

Contents

ACKNOWLEDGEMENTS

Many of those who knew and worked with Lutah Maria Riggs have contributed to this publication. Those who were in her office in the post-World War II years, Richard B. Nelson, Deming Isaacson and Joseph Knowles have all provided information as well as insight into her as a person and as a practicing architect. Her devoted friend, Katherine McMahon, Chairperson of the History Committee of the Montecito Association, has helped to clear up a variety of mysteries relating to Lutah's clients and her buildings.

The cataloging of Lutah Maria Rigg's extensive archives and drawings on permanent loan to the Architectural Drawing Collection of the University Art Museum, University of California, Santa Barbara, has been carried out by Lauren Bricker, Patricia Halloran, Pamela Post, Lisa Kaftan, Ann Wellman, and Elizabeth Mjelde.

As always, we are in great debt to the Los Angeles architectural photographer, Marvin Rand. He has provided us with new and revealing insight into Lutah's architecture.

Finally, my thanks goes to Paul Gray for his continual support for this study of one of America's distinguished woman architects.

—D.G.

The display type, "Lutahline," was designed by Judith Sutcliffe, The Electric Typographer.

Lutah Maria Riggs at the library of the "Ark," University of California, Berkeley, 1920.

1. The Early Years

WHEN THE *LOS ANGELES TIMES* ANNOUNCED: "BARON VON ROMBERG BUILDS AT Montecito"[1] on May 23, 1937, the article told not only of a costly project to be mounted during the heart of the Great Depression, but also of a project to be designed by a Santa Barbara woman architect, Lutah Maria Riggs.

Baron Maximilian von Romberg's new estate was comparable to the great country houses built in Southern California in the more opulent teens and twenties, those designed by such figures as George Washington Smith, Reginald D. Johnson, Gordon B. Kaufmann, Wallace Neff and Addison Mizner. The von Romberg house may well have been the last California pre-World War II villa clothed in the Spanish Colonial Revival image.

Lutah Maria Riggs was a natural choice as designer of the Baron's house and garden, for she had helped create many of the "great" country houses of the twenties when she worked as the chief designer for Santa Barbara architect George Washington Smith. Few women had entered the professions when Riggs graduated from the architecture program at the University of California at Berkeley in 1919. Professional women were still quite unusual, even in the casual California of the 1920s, yet Riggs became highly successful. She joined Smith's practice in the early twenties and her abilities as a designer and draftsperson contributed substantially to the firm's national reputation. She was on her own by the 1930s, creating such masterpieces as the von Romberg house and helping to establish the Colonialized version of the California ranch house.

Riggs turned to the design of film stage sets during the war years and produced such striking sets as those used in MGM's *Picture of Dorian Gray*. From the late 1940s on, she was a major participant in the West Coast renaissance of a woodsy version of Modernist architecture. In the final decades of her life (the 1960s and 1970s), she emerged as a leading figure in the return to traditionalism. Her Vedanta Temple in Montecito together with a number of her gardens and residential designs are key monuments in the history of late twentieth-century architecture on the West Coast.

In the practice of architecture, her approach fell into that longstanding tradition of the gentlewoman/gentleman designer. With the exception of her work in Los Angeles during the late 1930s and early 1940s, she operated her architecture practice from either her Montecito studio and home, or from the service quarters of the 1926–27 Johnson House on nearby Sycamore Canyon Road. As certainly was (and is) the case with many successful architects, she did not openly solicit commissions; prospective clients came to her.

Riggs's commissions were almost entirely domestic. Her office in Montecito, adjacent to Santa Barbara, removed her from the urban scene of Los Angeles with its continual demand for new large and small scale buildings. Though she was active in planning and architectural review in Santa Barbara and Santa Barbara County, she preferred not to join social or business clubs. She had little or no contact with the business world of Santa Barbara or Southern California, nor did she cultivate political figures in order to obtain commissions for public buildings. Although she had entered a handful of competitions in the twenties and thirties, she scrupulously avoided them in the prosperous years after 1945. Like her fellow Californian, Julia Morgan, Riggs devoted little time to "selling" her architecture through popular shelter magazines or professional architectural journals. She was active in the American Institute of Architects, but only out of a sense of obligation to her profession and not in a bid for prominence in the hope of obtaining commissions.

When discussing her childhood, Riggs would always mention the facts—she was born October 31, 1896 in Toledo, Ohio (her mother made up her name)—but she shied away from conveying any feelings about these early years. Her mother, Lucinda C. Barrett, and her father, Charles B. Riggs, were married in 1893. Her father had a modest practice as a physician in Toledo and Middletown, Ohio. In the late 1890s his health "broke down" as a result of lung disease, probably tuberculosis, and he decided that he could regain his health by moving to one of the dry regions of California. While his family remained in Ohio, Charles Riggs settled in Pasadena, California, but his health did not improve. Perhaps reaching out to a last resource, he became deeply involved in "The Esoteric Fraternity," one of numerous religious cults that have surfaced over the years in Southern California.[2] His letters to his wife reveal how a scientific mind changed to one with an almost completely emotional response to life and the world.

Charles Riggs's departure for California placed Lutah and her mother in difficult economic circumstances, out of which they were apparently helped by members of the Barrett family. Lucinda Riggs remained closely attached to her husband, but their letters indicate that he increasingly distanced himself from her and Lutah. Lucinda suggested that he might resume at least a limited medical practice in Pasadena and also that she and Lutah join him there. But, like other converts to esoteric sects, he seemed to have married into the cult, and Lucinda and Lutah remained in Ohio.

Charles Riggs died in Pasadena in August 1905, and shortly after, Lucinda remarried. Her second husband, Theodore Dickscheidt, remains at best a shadowy figure whom Riggs avoided mentioning. We do not know anything about his background, his occupation, or even when and where he and Lutah's mother were married. Lutah did mention that he traveled to Santa Barbara to seek employment, and that she and her mother joined him there in 1914.[3]

Lutah attended grammar school in Middletown, Ohio, then the family moved to Indianapolis where she attended Manual Training High School for four years. Copies of *The Booster*, the school publication, reveal that she was an active student and on the honor rolls.[4] One of her class notes for these high school years mention that she bought (or pretended to buy?) a lake shore lot in Michigan for which she designed a cabin.[5] A few drawings also survive from these high school years, but they do not suggest the talent she later developed as one of America's gifted architectural artists.

After arriving in Santa Barbara, Riggs enrolled in Santa Barbara Normal School, one of a number of state-sponsored schools organized to provide teachers. Reflecting a general interest in the need for a college education for women, Riggs compiled a two-page bibliography for one of her classes.[6] These articles, published in popular magazines during 1912, range from "Has College Really Helped Girls?" in an issue of *Ladies Home Journal*, to "Working One's Way Through College" in the *Review of Reviews*.[7] Riggs attended the Normal School for two years, and also worked part-time as a bookkeeper for the local Woolworth store.

In 1917, she won a scholarship to the University of California at Berkeley by selling the most subscriptions to the *Santa Barbara Daily News* in a contest. Riggs succeeded in prevailing upon the owner and publisher of the paper, Thomas Storke (who later became a U.S. Senator, a Regent of the University of California, and a close friend of Riggs's), to fully fund her studies for at least a year.

Riggs had kept desk calendars since her high school days, and she used them much like diaries.[8] While they reflect her activities during those early years, they contain very little about the historic events of those times. Other than to note a letter she wrote to the *Santa Barbara Daily News* on May 16, 1918,[9] Riggs's calendar makes no mention of the political and social events of the late 1910s, in particular, the First World War. Her calendar for November 11, 1918, is silent on the subject of the Armistice, nor are there any remarks about the brief economic depression that followed 1918.

Riggs's datebook indicates that she arrived in Berkeley on January 12, 1918, and quickly found a room. She began her architectural studies in the romantic, wood-shingled "Ark," a building designed in 1906 as a temporary building for the Architecture Department by John Galen Howard, who was both the chair of the department and architect for the campus.[10] Within a few days she was fully involved in the department's program, beginning by drawing orders, working on assigned En Loge and Esquisse projects, and later attending a lecture in French on the Belgian Art Nouveau architect Victor Horta.

Riggs's years at the Ark, 1918 to 1921, included three other women, Rose Luis, Irene McFall and Elah Hale. Judging by the entries in Riggs's day calendars, the four women were fully accepted into the social and educational affairs of the Ark, and the calendar records numerous parties, dances and social affairs. Most frequently mentioned in her calendars was fellow student Duke Wellington.[11] To leaven the long days, evenings and even nights spent working in the Ark, she and her friends saw such silent films as Mary Pickford's *How Could You Jean?* went on walks and hikes in Golden Gate Park, and on long treks north of the Bay in Marin County. Mindful that she was there on scholarship, Riggs also earned part of her keep by setting tables at the U.C. Berkeley Faculty Club.

*Fig. 1**

As were most architectural programs in the United States, Berkeley's was a direct outgrowth of the French Ecole des Beaux Arts program of teaching architecture. The department was not established until 1903, although architectural drawing had been taught earlier by Bernard Maybeck. The founding Chairman of the Department, and one of Riggs's close mentors, was John Galen Howard (1864–1931).[12] Howard had attended M.I.T. and later went to Paris to study at the Ecole.[13] Before opening his own office in New York with his partner Samuel A. Cauldwell, he had worked in the

**Figure numbers refer to illustrations beginning on page 46.*

offices of Henry Hobson Richardson and, later, of McKim, Mead and White.

Howard and Cauldwell entered the 1897 Phoebe Apperson Hearst International Competition for the new campus of the University of California at Berkeley. Though their scheme won fourth prize, Howard was appointed to the architecture advisory committee that was to help implement the winning plan by the French architect Emile Benard.[14] When Benard declined to come to Berkeley to supervise the building of the new campus, Howard was appointed campus architect in 1901 (a position he held until 1924) and became the founding Chair of the Department of Architecture in 1903. As an assistant, he brought in William Charles Hays, a graduate of the University of Pennsylvania and the Ecole, and he employed a number of practicing architects in the Bay Region to teach and criticize the students' work. While Riggs attended Berkeley, the visiting critics included Bernard Maybeck; Ernest Coxhead, an English architect who helped to establish the First Bay Tradition; John Bakewell, Jr., who, like Howard, was a sophisticated Beaux Arts designer; John Donovan, the architect of many schools throughout California; Walter Raymond Yelland, one of the gifted proponents of the Second Bay Tradition; and Warren C. Perry, one of Howard's first students and later a graduate of the Ecole des Beaux Arts.[15]

Though somewhat reserved and aloof, Howard was closely involved with the teaching program, and he was highly supportive of the best students, including Lutah Maria Riggs. While in the program Riggs studied the classical orders under William C. Perry, and she developed remarkable abilities as a deliniator working in water color, gauche and pen and ink with Valerie De Mari. The teacher whom Riggs felt closest to though was William Charles Hays. This close relationship continued after she left Berkeley, partly due to Hays' marriage to her friend and fellow student Elah Hale.[16]

Schools of architecture in America—Berkeley, Massachusetts Institute of Technology, Harvard, Pennsylvania, Cornell—all modeled their programs after the French Ecole des Beaux Arts.[17] The centerpiece was the studio, with its intense concern for the principles of design and the means of communication—drawing. Work in the studio was supplemented by lectures on construction and engineering, and on architectural history and theory. Hays and Howard taught the history and theory courses during Riggs's period at the Ark.

Summing up the goal of the Ecole, Howard wrote, "Freedom and sincerity, then, personal effort and self-dependency, guided by wise experience and knowledge of the past—these are the intellectual gifts most treasured at the school, which inculcates the principle that, if ours is to take rank with the great periods of art, we must not be content with taking material from other times and incorporate it, transmuted by personal effort, into structures, which by the very act, are deprived of life: but we must seize the character of our time, as the great artists that of theirs, and through travail of the spirit, work out into a living art."[18]

Students learned design by addressing architectural problems, and their solutions were critiqued by professors in the department and by visiting critic-architects, who were invited to comment on particular problems. At Berkeley the most common problems were either Esquisse, an informal sketch problem, or En Loge, the preparation of a preliminary design within a set time, usually a short period.

Figs. 2, 3, 4

Riggs noted a good number of these class problems in her calendars. The exercises provide a glimpse of the approach taken to building types, and the distinction between international classical design images and more regional images associated with the West Coast. Characteristic of the classical-oriented imagery was an Esquisse concerning an "Hermitage" (November 23, 1918), and a variety of En Loge problems ranging from "Monumental Fountain" (November 16, 1918), to "A War Memorial and Chapel" (September 25, 1919), and a "A Memorial to Irish Hope and Memory" (February 24, 1921). Contrasting to these classical-oriented projects were a number reflecting a regional interest: Esquisse problems entitled "A Suburban Station" (May 10, 1919), "A House on a Hill" (September 13, 1919), "A Gatehouse for a Reservoir" (November 8, 1919), "A Ranch House" (February 15, 1920), "A Rustic Bridge" (March 13, 1920), and En Loge exercises titled "A Tile Manufacturer" (March 25, 1920) and "A Gas Station and Halfway House" (March 31, 1921).

Supplementing the problems were required "Historical Drawings," measured, elevation or perspective drawings of the major monuments of the Classical/European tradition. These drawings were derived from existing, already published drawings and/or photographs. Historical drawings familiarized the students with the underlying design principles of the monuments and expanded the students' abilities in draftsmanship. Among Riggs's historical drawings are pen and inks (often accompanied by a watercolor wash) of French and English cathedrals, villas and townhouses of Italy, and rural country houses of England, France, Italy and Spain. Some major nineteenth-century works are also included, such as H.L. Elmes, Robert Rawlinson and C.R. Cockerell's 1851–54 St. George's Hall in Liverpool. Riggs graduated from the program in late May 1919, and continued graduate studies at the Ark, taking additional courses from Howard in theory and participating in a number of Esquisse and En Loge problems.

During her years at the Ark, Riggs often went to the hills above Berkeley to sketch, and she produced designs for posters, book plates, and book and cover designs. She quickly became an accomplished draftsperson, winning numerous prizes, the most important being the Alumni Prize (May 22, 1919), a prize which provided her with much needed financial help for her second year at the school. *Fig. 5*

She also gained experience and income with her production of drawings for others. Only some of her calendar entries describe the drawings she worked on in detail. For instance, on February 25, 1919, she simply noted that she had *"worked on drawings for Mrs. Boynton,"* without recounting the subject of the drawings.[19] Before she joined the Draftsman's Union in July 1919, she had done some drafting for the small San Francisco architectural office of Smith and Brian. Later in July she applied for a part-time position at the well-known firm of Weeks and Days, but was turned down. In August she began to do drafting for Riedel Building Corporation of Berkeley and San Francisco, and at the end of that month she was engaged by the San Francisco City Engineers Office to draw maps. Her first project was a new site map for the suburban development of St. Francis Woods (which had originally been laid out in 1912 by Olmsted and Olmsted, with John Galen Howard). Later, in 1920 and 1921, she laid out similar maps for the City Engineers office at Berkeley. *Fig. 6*

Early in the summer of 1920, Howard helped her obtain a drafting position in northeastern California, with the Susanville architect, Ralph D. Taylor. Though Susanville was a small community at the time (around 3,000 people), it was prosperous. Its *Fig. 7* largest industry was the Fruitgrowers Supply Company box factory, supplemented by lumber mills and other small industries, including tourism. The town was east of Lassen National Forest and midway between Eagle Lake to the north and Honey Lake to the south. Tourists from the Bay Region arrived regularly on the Reno-Susanville Branch of the Southern Pacific Railroad, and Howard came to visit Riggs in Susanville during a short vacation in Lassen National Forest in late August.

Fig. 8

Ralph D. Taylor's architecture office consisted of himself and Riggs. She would later say that one of the reasons she got the job was because she was a woman and could easily live with the Taylor family in their house. (She also stayed from time to time in a local hotel.) In contrast to the somewhat depressed economic conditions of urban California, there was a reasonable amount of building activity in and around Susanville.

Riggs arrived in Susanville on August 2, 1920, and her datebook shows that she was working on the drawings for a bath house the day after her arrival. Riggs worked on a wide variety of projects, ranging from the bath house to a county garage, an addition to a hospital, a public library, a "scheme for a bank," an apartment house, and a mountain lodge. Whether Riggs was a designer or simply drafted schemes given to her, we do not know. The only preserved drawings from her months in Susanville are sketches she made during her trips to Lassen National Forest. While working for Taylor in this small town, Riggs entertained herself by riding horses and visiting both the nearby National Forest and the surrounding lakes.

She returned to Oakland by train on December 4, 1920, and was promptly back at the Ark on December 6 producing an En Loge for a "Small City Bank." She then returned to the job-hunting trail, applying to Louis Christian Mullgardt (he was out of town, working on a project in Honolulu), and Julia Morgan, who gave "a halfway promise" to engage her. Her calendar for January 31, 1921 notes, *"received letter from Julia Morgan."* One can assume that Morgan's answer was negative, since Riggs continued to work on maps for the Berkeley City Engineer's office, producing among other things, "School Board Maps."

From early January through July she also continued to work for W.C. Riedel and she produced drawings to remodel the Sonoma County ranch house of Thaxter and Florence Thayer (which was not built).[20] At the invitation of Riedel, Bernard Maybeck visited the office at a time when Riggs was drawing a spec house in a somewhat loose medieval style. She recalled that Maybeck came over and looked at her drawings. In his usual kind and gentle fashion he commented that it ". . . looked like a house in the Black Forest, not for [the] Berkeley Hills."[21]

Fig. 9

Though Riggs was certainly disappointed with the job situation, the winter and spring of 1920–21 in Berkeley were happy and stimulating periods in her life. She had developed a close group of friends in Berkeley, and the Ark was even more active socially. John Bakewell, Jr. and Ernest Coxhead were critics at the Ark, and she twice met Bernard Maybeck. She also did some independent designs: a *"sketch for an Apartment House for Miss Buchan,"* sketches for a house for Tabor Sperry, and a design for a lamp.

By summer's end in 1921, Riggs had decided to return to Santa Barbara to find a drafting job there or in the Los Angeles area. In part this was due to her mother's poor health and financial needs. She often mentioned later that, while working in

Susanville, she had come across a 1919 publication containing an illustration of a George Washington Smith house. She had been impressed by the romanticism and abstraction of historic forms combined in the house, and she decided to seek a position in his office.

The publication she had seen was actually the October 1920 issue of the *Architectural Record*, in which Smith's own house (later the Heberton House) of 1916 was illustrated in a number of plates within a long article, "The American Country House," authored by the well-known East Coast architect, William Lawrence Bottomsley.[22]

Reading this article may have planted the idea of working with Smith among Riggs's aims, but after her return from Susanville, she was also seriously considering positions in the Bay area. Working with Smith was only one possibility of the several she had in mind at the time.

Riggs rejoined her mother in Santa Barbara on August 4, 1921, and was laying out a poster the next day at the design studio of Kem Weber for the Community Arts Association. Weber was associated with the retail and production firm of Barker Brothers in Los Angeles, and, at his suggestion, Riggs wrote to them concerning job possibilities.

A few days later, she interviewed at George Washington Smith's studio and residence in Montecito for a drafting position.[23] Smith already had two draftspersons in his office, but he also had a fair amount of work. Riggs said that Smith was impressed with the drawings she had brought along, but deferred making a decision for a few weeks. She concluded that his reticence in hiring her was because she was a woman, and because he was uncertain whether his present volume of work would continue.

She took the train to Los Angeles and spent a number of days visiting large and small architecture offices, including those of Robert D. Farquhar; H. H. Hewitt; Morgan, Walls and Morgan; Allison and Allison and Stiles Clements at the Meline Co.; and Carleton M. Winslow. She also inquired at the Hunt and Chambers office in the Hibernian Building in downtown Los Angeles and looked into designing stage sets for the Lasky Studios. The answer was always "No."

In Los Angeles she learned from a friend that Smith had only recently told other architecture firms that he needed another draftsperson. She returned to Santa Barbara on August 20 and, she noted in her calendar, *"Went to see Mr. Smith with some success."* The following day she wrote, *"Called Mr. Smith and decided to work for him."*

(Fig. 68) Lutah Maria Riggs at the C. Pardee Erdman house, Montecito, 1966.

II. In the Office of George Washington Smith

IT WOULD APPEAR FROM HER CALENDAR ENTRIES THAT THREE INDIVIDUALS WERE THEN working in the Montecito studio-office of Smith. These were a "Mr. Handy," L. Wass and Keith Lockard. At the moment Riggs entered the office, a *"Mr. Stacy, an English architect started to work* [the] *same time I did."* (Calendar, August 22, 1922). Her first task in the office was to do some of the details for the Mary Stewart House (Montecito, 1922). She also worked on some elevations for the three Maravilla Company spec houses in Ojai (1922–23), and she *"rendered* [a] *Country Club Sketch."* In mid-September Smith indicated that he did not seem to have enough work at the moment to keep her on, and he advised her temporarily to take a job teaching at the nearby Casitas Pass rural school—a position she had looked into before she was hired by Smith. *Figs. 10, 11*

It is difficult to sense exactly what was going on in the Smith office, and why he would, even on a temporary basis, be willing to lose Riggs. She left the office on October 1, 1921, and she opened the small one-room school with ten students on October 3. But she also continued to work in Smith's office, preparing among other drawings, a preliminary sketch for the George Steedman House. How she balanced teaching at Casitas Pass and work in the Smith office is difficult to ascertain, for she notes a number of days devoted to drafting which alternated with days teaching.[1]

Before she left for teaching she had proudly purchased her first automobile, a Chevrolet roadster, taking delivery of it on October 9. Though she continually notes recurring mechanical problems with the car and occasional minor accidents, it would seem that the roadster became a symbol of her freedom and control of her activities.

Though she did produce some working drawings during these early years in the office, it would appear that her contribution was that of a designer—ranging from working with Smith on the overall design of a building to producing many presentation and drawings of details. When asked late in her life about the way Smith worked with her on the office projects she said:

> *"Mr. Smith would come over to my drafting table and we'd talk about what we were going to do and I'd know about when he was coming out to talk with me and would probably have time to draw some scribbled sketches and then if he okayed them or added something to them or changed something and then I would hand those little sketches to* [one of the draftspersons]*, we had three draftsmen with us . . ."*[2]

By late 1921, she was, in essence, treated as a member of the Smith family. She and Smith went out to examine sites for projected buildings, and the two of them crawled around the old existing adobe Lobero Theater Building to obtain its measurements.

Riggs noted down on numerous occasions that she and Mary Smith or George had lunch or dinner together. She noted on July 22, 1922, *"Went with* [the] *Smiths in their Lincoln to Los Angeles. Ate lunch on the road. Stayed at the Alexander* [Hotel]*; went to the California* [Theater] *to see John Barrymore in "Sherlock Holmes."*

In early December 1922, the Smiths invited her to accompany them to Mexico. The purpose of the trip was to acquaint themselves more intensely with Mexican architecture, particularly domestic designs. They both purchased and took many photographs, made sketches, and noted down measurements of numerous details—iron work, stone door frames, balconies, and the like. She wrote on December 20, that *"Mr. Smith and I took a tour of patios* [in Puebla] *and measured one."* Alone or with the Smiths, Riggs traveled back and forth across central Mexico visiting Cuernavaca, Churubusco, San Angel, Coyoacan, Chapultepec, Puebla, Orizaba, Guadalupe, Queretaro, Guanajuato, Guadalajara, and other cities. In Mexico City, she and the Smiths met the Pasadena architect, Garrett van Pelt, and the Santa Barbara designer, Bert Harmer. Riggs and George Smith looked into manufacture of tiles which they could use in their own projects. Riggs was deeply impressed by the simplicity and abstract qualities of the Mexican domestic architecture. She was not sympathetic to the exuberance of the Churrigueresque Mexican churches. She wrote during her visit to Puebla, that *"Some of the churches are nice outside, but all are terrible inside. The entrance doors are nice, and some of the grill work."*[3]

The Smiths and Riggs arrived back in Santa Barbara on January 7th, and a few days later she noted that *"Lemrow and Benedict [were] fired"* from the Smith office and that Floyd E. Brewster and Harold Edmundson were engaged. During the late winter on through the summer, Riggs worked on a number of projects including the making of a model for the new Lobero Theater. Smith felt that it might be advantageous for his practice if they were to produce a volume of photographs, sketches and measured drawings of traditional Mexican architecture. The idea of such a publication had been on his mind when he organized the Mexican trip. The photographs, measurements, and the drawings which he and Riggs made were then thought of not only as a specific source which they could use in design, but also as the basis for a projected book. He was serious enough about the project to have Riggs spend considerable drafting time over several of the following months in preparing a number of measured and perspective drawings, but the press of normal work in the office prompted Smith to finally drop the project. During the year, Riggs also took off time for a visit to San Francisco and Berkeley.

Figs. 12, 13, 14, 15, 19, 20

In November 1924, encouraged by Smith, she entered a regional competition for "A Small House in Brick," costing less than $7,500.00. This competition with its monetary prizes was sponsored by California Common Brick Manufacturers and the two California Chapters of the A.I.A.[4] Riggs's design for a story and a half French Norman cottage won the fourth prize and $50.00.

Fig. 22

Her winning design was a further development of the scheme Smith and she had first proposed in September 1921 for the John D. Wright Beach cottage in Montecito. It served as well as the source for Smith's James R. H. Wagner house of 1923, in Montecito. Riggs sited the house, as Smith had with his first house of 1916, close to the road so that a private garden could be placed to the rear. In her plan, a story and a half living room was placed to the left, a dining room and stairs in the center, and a kitchen and garage to the right. The living room and the dining rooms opened onto the garden terrace through French doors. Upstairs, reached by a small wall-contained winding circular stairway was a carefully worked out plan for the two bedrooms accompanied by a dormer-lighted hall, a large bath, and walk-in closets.

The precedent of the small rural farm houses of northern France for designs of American dwellings was one of the popular Period Revival styles of the twenties.[5] The popularity of these stone and half-timber farm houses was to a considerable degree due to the familarity of many Americans with this area of France during the First World War (reinforced by a number of American films whose setting was in this area of France). Though she had not yet been to Europe, Riggs, with her Beaux Arts training, knew very well how to use the then available published photographs and drawings. Her perspective drawings for her prize house depict the dwelling as if it was located alongside a rural European road, and she reinforced this atmosphere by including a French farm woman approaching the entrance.

Since the street facade of the dwelling contained the more utilitarian aspects of the house, she was able to use long blank walls of brick, penetrated by only a few carefully disposed openings. The composition builds itself up from left to right: the low street wall of the living room fronts the center section which is a story and a half and is penetrated by more openings. Finally the right section was composed of a deeply set-in garage entrance, above which was a cantilevered second floor of half-timbering (with the first floor wall plane of brick running uninterrupted from one end of the house to the other).

Not withstanding this carefully composed composition, the dwelling radiates (as did Smith's own first house) the elements of charm, character and romance (particularly the latter) which were so much sought after in the decades of the 1920s and 1930s.[6] All nine of the winning drawings submitted to the Competition were well rendered, but hers is by far the most individual and impressive rendering of the group. Though based upon a perspective drawing done on the drafting board, Riggs's drawing has the feel of a loose freehand sketch, perhaps closer to a drawing as "art" than a depiction meant solely to convey architectural intent. Her apparent looseness of technique and the gentle or staccato curling and swirling lines, which so beautifully convey the sense of romance, were the qualities which very quickly established her as one of America's foremost delineators of the twenties.[7] But these non-Beaux Arts qualities may well have made the jury feel a bit uneasy.

Riggs's submission in the Common Brick Competition should probably be treated as her first independent design. As such it displays a remarkable ability on her part to be able to absorb and then apply the lessons learned from her Beaux Arts training and from her exposure and sympathetic response to Smith and his highly painterly, abstract approach to design. She was then only 27 years old, and already she had arrived as a mature designer.

Her second independent commission of the twenties was her own house "Clavelitos," up Middle Road from the Smith house and studio-office (1926).[8] Smith helped her with funds to purchase the land and to finance the dwelling. Her first sketches were for a one-story Andalusian farm house, with a high central gabled roof section, off which to each side were shed roof extensions. The plan was that of a large story and a half combined living and dining room, with a kitchen appendage and

Figs. 23, 24, 25

then a guest room to one side, and a bedroom to the other. She eventually went on to a two story scheme—the living room being a full two stories high, a guest room over dining area and kitchen, and a bedroom to one side.

The site plan provided for the narrow end of the house to face the street with an exterior staircase—so that guests could come and go without going through the house. A two car garage and the west wall of the house defined a small auto court. Entrance to the house was through an arched gateway which led into a small formal garden. The thick wall surfaces of the dwelling were the prime ingredients of the design; their carefully defined proportions and the accents of a few windows and doors (all deeply set within the walls) reiterated the same qualities of abstraction found in the designs then coming from the Smith office.

In November 1924 Riggs and the Smiths went on one of their long trips—in this instance to Spain, France and England. As usual they both made drawings and took photographs of buildings which they felt might be consulted for their own designs. In Spain they spent some time with Arthur Byne and Mildred Stapley; they obtained samples of tile and photographs from ARXIV "Mas" in Barcelona. A similar trip was planned in 1928, but Smith did not feel well, so Lutah went with her friend, Helen Rearwin. This study trip took them again to Spain, to the gardens and villas of Italy, and to the rural buildings in France, Germany, and Swizerland. Thus by the end of the decade Riggs had fully supplemented her formal education at Berkeley and her several years of practice with George Washington Smith with the much needed exposure to Europe's traditional architecture.

Fig. 21

In the mid-twenties the Smith office consisted of Riggs, Floyd Brewster, Harold Edmondson, Douglas Honnold, and Hilma Tyson.[9] The group often ate lunch together in the adjoining courtyard, and while the group was close knit, it did not seem to have the camaraderie which Riggs had experienced as a student in the Ark. Perhaps, in part, this was due to the close relationship between Riggs and the Smiths—she was not only the principal designer, but was treated as an intimate member of the family, traveling with them and being invited to their many dinner parties.

As the drawings from the Smith office indicate, Riggs seldom did the working drawings for the various projects. Smith discussed with her the approach which a design should take, and on occasion provided her with small sketch drawings of a site plan, floor plans, elevations. She then organized this material into sketches, which she again went over with Smith; these were followed by small scale (usually ⅛ inch) measured drawings, and finally one or more perspective drawings.

In the later stages of a project Riggs would often provide the drawings (many at full scale) for details such as the iron work, tile patterns, woodwork and the like. As the Smith records indicate, he frequently would select details from one of his books and suggest that these be used as the point of departure for the design of a fireplace, a stairway, or a door frame. In some instances, he simply left it to Riggs to come up with her own sources and resulting design. This was the case for the interior columns and capitals in the Lobero Theater in Santa Barbara (1922–24) whose design was derived from a plate in Andrew N. Prentice's *Renaissance Architecture and Ornament in Spain*.[10]

For some smaller projects she was left on her own. The design for the Wayside Drinking Fountain in Sycamore Canyon, Santa Barbara (1926), for Mrs. Geoffrey

Courtney, was essentially an independent design of hers. In the 1970s, when she discussed this design, she indicated that she showed Smith her design (which he approved of) and that he gave her completely free rein to work out the concept and the final design.

In addition to work in the Smith office, Riggs produced for herself designs for wood frame, canvas garden umbrellas (a version being currently produced today under the name of "Santa Barbara umbrellas"), posters for Santa Barbara's annual fiestas, Christmas cards, book plates, and many sketches from nature.

One of the recurring historical problems which often crops up in the practice of architecture is who in fact was responsible for the designs coming from an office. Within the history of architecture there are a number of instances when brilliant younger designers have worked with major "name brand" figures. Two cases in point would be Joseph Gandy and his work in the office of Sir John Soane and Stanford White in the office of Henry Hobson Richardson. There is no question that both Gandy and White were gifted designers, and it is quite evident that they contributed in a substantial way to the products which came from their respective offices. It is equally evident though that the designs emanating from the Soane and Richardson offices were the products of their principals.

Riggs's relation with Smith was of a similar order. She absorbed what he was about as an architect, and she then contributed to his designs in a substantial way. Though Smith was trained both as an architect and fine art artist, his drawings, rather surprisingly, are not very good. What he intended in his buildings is evident in his drawings, but the drawings have no life of their own in strong contrast to those of Riggs, which often end up as being works of art in themselves. The essence of Smith's highly abstract approach to design was forcefully asserted in his first 1916 house, and such later, pre-Riggs designs as the Courtney House, Montecito (1921–22) or the Stewart House in Montecito (1921–23).[11]

Though the essential design concepts were his, Smith was well aware that the final designs owed much to Riggs's participation. When she entered the Smith office in 1921 she was employed as far as the office records indicate as a "junior" draftsman. By 1924 she had officially become a partner and the chief draftsman of the small firm. Riggs had received her California architectural license in 1928, and Smith tended even more than before to rely upon her design abilities. In late 1929, he began discussing with Riggs a change in his practice, in which she would become a full partner. When the stock market crash occurred late that year, their office had a number of projects on the board, including a large house for the film director/producer Samuel Goldywn (1928–29). Then, on the 16th of March, 1930, Smith died suddenly from a heart attack. Though Riggs and Harold Edmondson formed a partnership which continued Smith's practice, it turned out to be a winding down operation, in part due to the disappearance of Smith, who was almost entirely responsible for obtaining the commissions, and equally it was a result of the negative economic impact of the Great Depression.

(Fig. 20) Conte crayon drawing for GWS for Fagan/Crocker house, Pebble Beach, 1927-30.

III. Lutah Maria Riggs on her own in the 1930s

The partnership with Harold Edmondson did not turn out to be a pleasant affair from Riggs's point of view, and it came to an end just before January 1931.[1] Riggs felt that Edmondson had little to offer other than his ability as a draftsman, and there was more than a hint that he felt a male superiority over women. Riggs continued to enjoy a close personal relationship with Mary Smith as well as to use George's studio-office at the house. Mary Smith, according to Riggs, did not get along well with Edmondson, and she urged Riggs to dissolve the partnership.[2]

In addition to the Goldwyn house, there were a number of other Smith projects which never came to realization in 1930. Among these were the E. A. Oviatt House, Santa Barbara (1929–30) and the William S. Fairchild House, Montecito (1929–30). Projects which did go forward to completion were the Henry Culley House, Montecito (1929–30) and the Henry Eichheim Beach House at Sandyland (1929–30). In addition, there were several commissions for additions to earlier Smith residences, plus the final tile work on the Santa Barbara Cemetery Crematorium (Santa Barbara, 1924–25; 1932).

Of these, the most charming was the small gem of an octagonal library which Riggs designed for the George Steedman house (Montecito, 1929–33).[3] This small library was projected at a 45 degree angle from the northeast corner of the living room. A narrow passage leads into the eight-foot-wide room, and the interior soars upward into a small ribbed dome. Externally, Riggs purposely hid the new addition so that it would not intrude on the north or east elevation of the house, nor would it compromise the adjoining walled Spanish garden to the east. *Fig. 27*

There were two commissions which had entered the Smith office early in 1930. These were the William H. Andrews House (Montecito, 1930) and the J. Wesley Gallagher House (Montecito, 1930–31). Riggs provided the entire design for these two houses. Both were Andalusian Spanish, similar in concept to Smith's late twenties design, as well as having overtones of scale and fenestration derived from Riggs's own house of 1926. As with other architects across the country, the years 1931 and 1932 proved to be lean years for Riggs. There were a few additions and remodelings, a guest cottage in Montecito for Mrs. Lester Baldwin (1931) and a tremendous number of sketches and drawings for the unrealized residence for Mrs. Ellis Fischel in Montecito (1931). *Figs. 28, 29, 30, 31*

In the design for the Fischel house, guest house and garages, Riggs turned to the realm of Art Deco imagery. Though one does not associate this fashionable popular moderne image of the Art Deco with the Smith office, there were several projects for houses in this mode, the most interesting being the projected design for a retreat for *Figs. 32, 33*

Templeton Crocker at Pebble Beach (1927–30). In the Fischel design, Riggs turned to the more classical phase of the Art Deco. The flat-roofed stucco house displayed monumentality, countered by smaller scaled details associated with the English Regency style of the early nineteenth century. Among the several schemes for the Fischel Guest House was one which exhibited a central two story octagon with two identical wings to each side. Each of these wings were terminated by semi-circular ends, partially encased in glass brick. As in the design of the house, the central pavilion was defined by fluted walls which read as abstracted classical pilasters.

Most of 1932 and 1933 were spent working with her old friend, landscape artist A. E. Hanson in Los Angeles, first, on completing the West Adams Boulevard gardens of Mrs. Daniel Murphy, and later at the Palos Verdes estates.[4] For the Murphy Garden, *Figs. 34, 35, 36* she designed the upper and lower fountains and the dominant water cascade, the principal wall fountain, and various walls, balustrades and parapets. Riggs's calendars reveal that she had become a classic Southern California commuter over the month driving her car back and forth between Los Angeles, Palos Verdes and Santa Barbara.

Though the Depression had hit real estate severely, the Vanderlip family of New York (Frank Vanderlip, Sr. and Frank Vanderlip, Jr.), who had initiated the original development of the Palos Verdes peninsula in 1913, still wished to go ahead and complete the golf course and then lay out the second and third community centers (the first community center, Malaga Cove had been built between 1922–25). During one of her frequent work sessions in Palos Verdes she wrote:

> *"It was a perfect day and the ocean was as blue as the Mediterranean—I felt that Los Angeles could at length distinguish herself—with a place of such rare beauty as Palos Verdes showed herself to be that day it would make L.A. rank with all the best of the Riviera and the vicinity of Ravello and Amalfi. I hope that I am allowed to create some beautiful buildings there."*[5]

To provide a background for the Palos Verdes development, Hanson encouraged Riggs to visit the coastal development of Emerald Bay near Laguna Beach and also Avalon on Catalina Island. She liked what she saw at Emerald Bay and she took a number of photographs. At Catalina, she liked the casino and the buildings for the golf course, but overall she was not impressed. "[I] *think Catalina* [is a] *beautiful island, but very mercenary in* [its] *development*."[6] For Hanson, Riggs proceeded to design the various buildings of the golf course (1932). She designed a second plaza (1932, not built), laid out sections of residential lots, and designed a group of apartment houses (1932, not built).

Working from the old Smith office in Santa Barbara, she submitted a 1,600-foot house scheme (1932) to the Small House Bureau (with hopes that the working drawings for the scheme would be purchased and that the drawings would be published in the Bureau's magazine, *The Small Home*). On February 27, 1932, she wrote to *Good Housekeeping* magazine to see if its editors would be interested in having her do a *Fig. 37* house plan for them to be published in their series, "Studio of Architecture and Furnishings," edited by Helen Koues. Later the same year she submitted drawings to *House Beautiful*. Neither of these designs were published. The houses designed for these two magazines were in their imagery Spanish Colonial, with a two-story porch which suggested both Mexican prototypes, as well as California's Monterey tradition.

During her many trips and stayovers in the Los Angeles area, she recorded seeing a good number of the current films: *Hell Dives* with Wallace Berry and Clarke Gable, and *Lovers Courageous* with Robert Montgomery and Madge Evans, among them. She also went to concerts of the Los Angeles Philharmonic and to a number of plays. On May 31, 1932, she attended an exhibition. *"Saw Picasso, Derain, Dufy, Matisse exhibition at* [the] *Library. Seems all very superficial now somewhat think these canvases are poorest of these men left over to send on tour mostly abstractions, etc."*[7]

The years 1933 and 1934 were sparse in commissions, most of them being remodels and small additions to earlier Smith buildings. The one appreciable project, which was realized, was the Allen Breed Walker House on Hot Springs Road in Montecito (1934–35). The three components of this design were the house itself, a guest gatehouse, and a service building. Though the house was formal and grand in its detailing, it was not large. Its single floor centered on a large central living room which opened out onto a raised south-facing terrace though French doors. The style was late 18th-century French, a style that been used for interiors on several Smith houses.[8] Facing onto the road was a low stone wall which curved into the angled gate. Adjacent to the south side of the gate is the low stone guest house, with its wall dormer penetrating its mansard roof. The main stucco sheathed house seems more a modest garden pavilion overlooking its extensive terrace than a house. As in a good number of her later designs, Riggs laid out the grounds as well as planning the house.

Figs. 38, 39, 40, 41

During the following two years, 1936–1937, Riggs traveled back and forth between Santa Barbara and Los Angeles. There were as usual a number of remodelings and additions, and also an array of houses that were planned, but not built. While there were a few Spanish designs among these projects, most looked to late 18th century French architecture, to the Monterey tradition, to the English and American Georgian precedent, and to variations on the Anglo-Colonial revival, including the Regency. The French Provincial image was employed in her Edgar Davey House, Los Angeles (1935), and in the completed Leon Graves House, Sherman Oaks (1935–36). The Davey house, with its garage close to the street and its walled entrance court, is suburban in concept, while the Graves house is a miniaturized French country estate with a walled auto court, outbuildings and garages.

Fig. 45

Riggs's principal commission of the 1930s, and perhaps the most important design in her entire career, was the Baron Maximilian von Romberg Villa and Estate in Montecito (1937–38).[9] While there were some quite large houses and gardens designed in the Depression years of the 1930s in Southern California by Paul R. Williams, Gordon Kaufmann, Reginald D. Johnson, John Byers (with Edla Muir), Wallace Neff, and Roland E. Coate, the atmosphere of most of these houses tended to convey a smallness of scale and intimacy.

Along with the von Romberg house, there were a few houses of the period which carried on the scale of design one associates with the 1920s. Examples of these would be Wallace Neff's Italian Renaissance villa, the Henry F. Halseman House, Holmby Hills (1939) and his Mediterranean inspired, Enrique Schondube House in Bel Air (1936) and Roland E. Coate's Doric columned Jack Warner House in Beverly Hills (1926). Closer to Montecito, at the east end of the ocean front of Santa Barbara, was

Reginald D. Johnson's late 18th century derived Clark House (1932–36).

The clients for this palatial new dwelling were the 37-year-old Baron Maxmillian von Romberg, and his wife Emily Hall. Von Romberg, who died in a crash of his sports plane before the house was completed, was a passionate flyer and sportsman.[10] Riggs's notes and sketches for the von Romberg house portray a close involvement of both Maximilian and Emily in its design.

The rich array of sketches and perspective drawings for the von Romberg house illustrate the wide variety of strikingly different designs and images which were considered by Riggs and her pair of clients, Maximilian and Emily von Romberg.[11] First, the siting of the house on this 3.38 acre irregular "L-shaped" property posed two major of problems—how to preserve privacy from the adjoining two roads and also how to keep the building far enough back from the various property lines. Riggs provided four different schemes, and she and her clients finally arrived at the one which placed the houses near Hot Springs Road, and thereby opened up a large area to the northwest for a very private garden.

There were at least some twenty designs drawn up for the house, some of which were explored in only one or two tiny sketches, others of which were examined in careful measured drawings or even in large sized perspective drawings.[12]

The first scheme (numbered 4) starts off as a Palladian cruciform plan with a central octagonal room which rose two stories with a balcony around the second floor. This design was then elaborated with wings off the ends of the cross, forming a loose swastika. Externally the design centered on a three story crenelated medieval keep. The flavor of the design is that of a castellated late 15th-century country villa from northern Italy. This design, labeled by Riggs as the "Swastika Scheme" (based on the American Indian and Far Eastern swastika design), enclosed the arms of the swastika via walls and pergolas to form four enclosed courtyards.

Fig. 46

For Schemes 5 and 6, only floor plans remain (in a classic Beaux Arts fashion, she almost always started with the site plan and then plans for the project itself). These schemes were both most likely a classical Italian Renaissance design. Scheme 5 has a central entrance hall which runs through the house and then a pair of halls perpendicular to each side. A recurring theme in a number of the Scheme 6 designs was a circular reception room towards the front and a loggia and the major rooms facing onto a terrace to the back of the house.

The next two schemes, 8 and 9, (again only plans, no elevations) loosened up the earlier Italian designs into a more picturesque composition. The next scheme, no. 10, somewhat regularized the plans of 8 and 9. Elevational drawings indicate that the image then being thought about was Venetian/Byzantine. Perhaps the Byzantine image of George Washington Smith's Crocker-Fagan House (Pebble Beach, 1927–29) was being thought of. As in the earlier Scheme 3, the house centered on a three-story square medieval keep. The split curved crenelation at its top was a visual device usually associated with Islamic architecture. The castlelike atmosphere of the design is reinforced by the entire second floor roof being parapeted and crenelated in a fashion similar to the keep.

Fig. 47

The groups of drawings marked as schemes 10 through 15 set forth a really bewildering array of different design ideas. First (no. 10) is one called "Modern Classic," a variation on the theme of English Regency architecture. This is followed by

Fig. 48

a drawing bearing the designation "Modern." This interpretation of the Moderne is Art Deco in feeling, flat-roofed rectangular volumes with coined corners and regency fenestration. In the packet of scheme 11 drawings are first a Spanish Colonial revival design, then a series of flat roof moderne designs. The Moderne designs exhibit curved walls, corner windows, and the use of glass brick.

Scheme 12 swings back to the theme of the three-story medieval keep, only in this case the plan is arranged (in part) around an enclosed courtyard with loggias overlooking it on the second floor. The two images suggested are Spanish Colonial Revival and the northern Italian country house. Scheme 13 looks again at the Greek Cross or the swastika. The Greek Cross plan suggests a square open court and surrounding two story loggia in the center.

The first sheets of Scheme 15 take us back to the theoretical sketches of Eric Mendelsohn and Kem Weber in the late teens. The circle, as a modernist theme, was explored in this scheme: one with the house being a low cylinder, with a service wing off to one side; another being three cylinders, a large central cylinder with a center circular staircase, and then two circular wings to each side. Another modernist approach in one of the other schemes displayed a Y-shaped plan, with a circular central stair hall, and a square living room fitted between two arms of the Y. The final design is a Greek cross, with a circular low central keep. The extensive blank walls, and refined detailing of this scheme hint at the early 19th century regency one associates so closely with the work of Soane and Gandy.

Finally, in Scheme 16, we come to the germ of the house as built. The Italian-Spanish flavor is retained and so, too, such features as the three-story keep. Entrance to the house is gained via a door in the north wing which leads into an open loggia which overlooks a walled courtyard. The question pursued in these and other more detailed drawings is how much to retain of historical references and how much to suggest the plain geometric simplicity of the moderne. *Fig. 49*

The keep remained, but now was devoid of crenelation; the roofs are flat and parapeted; and the walls read as expansive light surfaces broken by only a few penetrations. The cantilevered hood over the entrance has gone from a design which was quite specific in its reference to northern Italian Romanesque examples to a striking, simple abstraction. The interior of the house evoked the sensitivity of the then popular Regency mode. The one major exception was the exercise/retreat room within the upper reaches of the keep. Its story and a half space, reminiscent of Le Corbusier's version of the Parisian artist's studio, was pure Streamline Moderne. *Fig. 50* *Fig. 51*

The sophisticated interior decor and furnishi ng were provided by one of America's foremost exponents of the Art Deco and Streamline Moderne, Paul Frankl. Riggs had tried to prevail upon the von Rombergs to engage A.E. Hanson to do the gardens, but she was not successful.[13] The landscape of existing trees, augmented by new planting, was well carried out, but the design of the gardens was not on the same level as that of the house. *Figs. 52, 53*

At the same time she was involved with the design of the von Romberg House, she utilized the Moderne image for a store building "Astor," to have been built on State Street in Santa Barbara for the Burke sisters (1936–37; 1946). One of the early schemes for the Montecito country house for Kent K. Parrot (1937) looked to a combination of the Streamline Moderne, coupled with a pared down version of "Hollywood" Regen- *Fig. 54* cy.[14] For Mrs. John C. Breckenridge's site, high on Mission Ridge overlooking Santa Barbara, she designed a C-shaped English Regency dwelling (not built, 1937–38). Projecting off one end of the C was the large living room with an apse end and extensive bay window to the front. The garage terminated the other end of the C, and a dining room occurred at the rear and center of the C.

At the request of the Santa Barbara Mutual Building and Loan Association, Riggs submitted a design for a small dwelling of less than one thousand square feet (1938). Her Colonial, somewhat Regency design was followed through preliminary drawings, but the final working drawings and the project itself were never carried out or the projected model house built. The Regency style was also employed for a two story house for Roland F. Woodyatt in Evanston, Illinois (unbuilt, 1938–40).

Though most of Riggs's designs of the late 1930s utilized non-Hispanic images, she still retained her fondness for the Mediterranean mode. In the early spring of 1940 she wrote a series of articles (at the behest of Pearl Chase) for the *Santa Barbara News-Press* on the subject of "Mediterranean Influence." The first of these articles dealt with the question of sources, the second with what she considered to be the greatest of the Mediterranean villas in Santa Barbara, the Gillespie house designed by Bertram G. Goodhue.[15] In the first of these articles she openly admitted the mythical nature of the Mediterranean in Santa Barbara:

Fig. 55

> *"When we speak of Mediterranean architecture of Santa Barbara, it is those regional roots we think of as belonging, if we stop to think. Along about the first of August every year* [when Santa Barbara holds its Fiesta], *we can't do much analytical thinking because our emotions tell us that Santa Barbara is Mediterranean Spanish only by grace of the Conquistadores. Then, for a spell, we ignore all the lesser influences and let Spain have her day."*

In mid-1937 Riggs was contacted by Newton Jackson of Los Altos. He was acquainted with George Washington Smith's impressive interpretation of the Spanish in the Jackling House (Woodside, 1925), and he wished her to design a two-story adobe dwelling which would reflect the character of a typical rural Mexican hacienda. The proportions of the walls, of the parapet roofs, together with the scale of the windows, and the thick piers of the corridors in this project thoughtfully reflect what she had experience in her 1922 trip to Mexico with the Smiths (only a section of the house was built).

Much of the time between 1929 and 1940 Riggs was involved with A. E. Hanson and the development of the equestrian-oriented suburban community of Rolling Hills. From 1939 through 1940 she was the consulting architect in Residence. This gated development comprised a section of the upper hills of the Palos Verdes Peninsula.[16] This land was to have been part of the original grand scheme which had been drawn up in the teens by Olmsted and Olmsted for the New York financier, Frank Vanderlip, Sr. and his associates (Palos Verdes Corporation). The name Rolling Hills was selected by A. E. Hanson for this new development in 1934, and the actual design and layout of the site took place in 1935, under the general direction of the planner Charles H. Cheney and A. E. Hanson (who from 1932 through 1941 was general manager of the Palos Verdes Corporation).

The concept behind the scheme for Rolling Hills was to create small "rancheros" of ten acres or more. Some of these ranchettes would be for weekend or summer use, other might be year round dwellings. As with the earlier Palos Verdes development in the twenties, restrictions were placed on the land use and architecture. Dwellings and other buildings were to be essentially one story high, and the image was to be that of the mid nineteenth-century California ranch house, somewhat "improved" by references to the popular Anglo-Colonial revival style.

Hanson initially engaged Paul R. Williams and James R. Friend to design the first buildings constructed at Rolling Hills between 1935 and 1938. With the marked upturn in building activity in the Los Angeles in 1939, Hanson asked Riggs to join him. She, together with Paul R. Williams, designed a number of Williamsburg—inspired single floor Colonial Revival house for Williamsburg Lane, and other parts of Rolling Hills. *Figs. 56, 57*

Eighteen of her 1939 designs were for projects in Rolling Hills. Of these eight were built. They range in size from a small cottage for Joseph A. Denni to larger houses designed for Edward C. Dudley, to a spec house designed for A.E. Hanson. A few of the designs were for Hollywood celebrities, such as the small Colonial house which she designed for Greta Garbo (1939).[17] Though these white clapboard single floor dwellings were, according to an advertisement, ". . . direct architectural descendants of the famous homes of eighteenth century Virginia," they were in fact versions of the then emerging fashion of the California ranch house.[18]

The design of these modest-sized, single story houses constructed in Rolling Hills in the late 1930s/early 1940s mirrored the popularity of this house type all over America. In the Northeast, the general commitment was to variations on the theme of the Cape Cod cottage, romantically realized in the work of the Boston architect, Royal Barry Wills.[19] On the West Coast the Colonialized ranch house came about in the late 1920s. William W. Wurster and Gardner Daily espoused the Colonialized ranch house in northern California.[20] In Los Angeles, H. Roy Kelley, Roland E. Coate and others designed many of these single-story or story-and-a-half ranch houses throughout the Los Angeles area.[21] Cliff May, whose name became synonymous with the popular California Ranch house in the pre- and post-World War II years, slowly transformed his more Hispanic ranch houses into a mode which was also more Colonial and more Moderne.

The Rolling Hills Colonial designs of Paul R. Williams, James Friend and Lutah Maria Riggs had plans organized around porches and terraces for out-of-door living, extensive use of glass French doors and bay windows, lowpitched roofs, and the garages often given great importance. Up to this time Riggs had not visited Williamsburg and Tidewater Virginia, but she had traveled to the southeast and down to New Orleans. These visits, together with the use of illustrations and drawings contained in the current architectural journals provided her with what she needed to know about this image. *Fig. 58*

On April 6, 1940 she wrote in her datebook, "*These periods of change and readjustment are certainly hard on the 'top and body.' My work is tapering to a close in Rolling Hills, as the sales there are few and far between now but my work is starting again in Santa Barbara all transitions are difficult, I suppose, but I find that, to keep my work at top notch at both ends of the line and at the required pace of production to keep all clients happy means extending myself to the limit. But I have to do it to keep going. At the same time I marvel at the flexibility of my transportation. Suppose I suddenly couldn't do all this travel? When that happens, I just can't even operate as I am now doing, that's all! I will feel very cramped, I am sure, after the ease and freedom I now enjoy."*[22]

During 1940 she continued her work at Rolling Hills, and she also designed two Monterey style residences: the two-story dwelling for Mrs. Charles H. Davis on the Riviera of Santa Barbara (1940–41) and the Mattie Ramelli House in San Bernardino (1940–41). For the Santa Barbara Botanical Gardens she provided a Library and Herbarium which posed as an informal fragment of a California Ranch house (1942).

Figs. 59, 60

Fig. 61

Riggs's calendar for 1941 provides one with a glimpse of how she worked professionally and what occurred in her daily life. As in the past, she was fond of attending the latest Hollywood films, concerts, art exhibitions (a showing of works by Cezanne and Picasso at the Los Angeles County Museum, February 18th), and stage plays, both in Los Angeles and in Santa Barbara. She had been elected President of the Santa Barbara Chapter of the A.I.A. so she attended the 73rd Convention of the A.I.A. which was held that year in Yosemite National Park (May 17–20). As the local President, she organized a post-Convention tour of Santa Barbara and Montecito. One of the participants at the A.I.A. meeting who also visited Santa Barbara, was Marion I. Manley, an architect who practiced in Coral Gables, Florida. She wrote Riggs after her California visit, *"They* [the members at the meeting] *actually thought, before you turned up at Yosemite, that I was the first and only woman Chapter President . . ."* As it turned out Marion and Riggs were indeed the first women architects to be Chapter Presidents.

During the latter part of the year she corresponded with Gordon B. Kaufmann, who at that time was President of the Los Angeles Chapter of the A.I.A. Kaufmann came up to Santa Barbara on October 3, 1941. Riggs wrote, *"Gordon Kaufmann came to call and to discuss the state of things. He has great faith—I feel perhaps a little too much—to be realistic. He doesn't seem to think we will be in the war."*[23]

With some of her commissions in Los Angeles and some in Santa Barbara, she continued as a classic Southern California commuter, often going back and forth from Santa Barbara to Los Angeles in one day. Though she had only a few commissions, it is quite apparent that she found it difficult to carry them all out within the time frame which was expected by many of her clients. A case in point would be the house which she was designing for Genevieve and William Keighley overlooking Toluca Lake in North Hollywood. She had been working with them since the late winter; they had gone to New York. Riggs was to arrange for grading and improvements to take place on their property so that when they returned in June all would be ready to start the house. On May 15th, she wrote to Genevieve:

> *"You may regard this letter as a receipt in full, for payment of my professional advice and services with respect to your proposed residence at Toluca Lake. It is my intention, in this way, to somehow make it up to you for the inconvenience I caused by failing to get the revised plan to you, and to get the retaining wall constructed before you returned from the East . . . I am full of blame, and defeat. Defeat, because you put in my lap the kind of house I have wanted for years to build, and I missed it."*[24]

As Riggs pointed out in her letter to Genevieve Keighley, the increased involvement of the United States in the Second World War made it increasingly difficult to obtain the one or two draftspersons she needed and also structural engineers. In Southern California, draftspersons and engineers were being absorbed into the many war industries. Equally though, it had to do with the way that Riggs was practicing architecture; her practice tended to be a one-person operation. She carried out the many needed site visits, selected all of the hardware, lights and other manufactured components of the project. Added to this was the time consumed in travel back and forth between Los Angeles and her home and commissions in Santa Barbara. Travel down to Rolling Hills and back, visits to such distant points as San Bernardino (the Ramelli House, 1940–41) consumed time as well.

Returning to her letter to Genevieve Keighley, one can sense her frustration:

> *"And even though I ended each day with a sense of frustration, nervous tension and worry, I determined, for the morrow, to get the outside work done early, so that I would have a nice uninterrupted afternoon and evening to sit down and concentrate on your work. Always something unexpected came on the morrow to destroy the plan. This went on daily like a treadmill."*[25]

Her calendar page for December 7th, 1941, has a notation at the top of the page *"War,"* followed by *"Warm and sunny—Perfect day."* In the days that followed Pearl Harbor she continued her then normal routine, including frequent trips to Los Angeles to inspect work in progress. Though there were a few projects worked on in 1942—alterations to the Ravencroft Ranch House in Goleta and the completion of her first group of buildings at the Santa Barbara Botanic Gardens, most of the nonwar oriented building activity pretty well ceased.

Both to contribute to the war effort and simply to make a living she began to inquire into aircraft and other defense industries in Los Angeles to see if she could obtain a drafting poistion. She talked with Paul Williams and others, and was just about to take a position when she heard from her old friend William Horning. He asked her whether she would be interested in joining the design staff of MGM. Friends who had been involved with the motion picture industry advised against it *". . . it might go to my head to be so close to the movies might get spoiled . . ."*[26]

She finally decided to see what it would be like, and Horning arranged an interview with Cedric Gibbons. In her entry for September 14, 1942, she wrote of the interview: *"Mr. Gibbons is dark and Irish quiet and so reserved seemed like Mr. Smith somewhat he looked at everything* [Riggs had brough a selection of her drawings and photographs of her work], *and said when could I start . . ."*[27] She then arranged to rent her Montecito house and obtained an apartment close to the studios in Culver City.

By mid-October she had started on her career as a film set designer. She continued through the war years to work for MGM and later for Warner Brothers through early 1945. Certainly, the best known of her set designs of these years was for the 1943 film, *The Picture of Dorian Gray*.[28] The story of Oscar Wilde took place in London in the early decades of the nineteenth century so she then had the then fashionable Regency Revival style opportunity. *Figs. 62, 63, 64*

While working on the designs for this film she went back and reread the story. In her datebook of 1943 she laid down her ambivalence about the story itself, and the approach between taken to it as a Hollywood film.

> *"I was still working on* Dorian Gray *when I caught the flu. I have enjoyed this almost more than anything else I have done at MGM regardless of whether it becomes a good movie or not. The director of acting is Lewin new at the lot, but with a fine record as a director. I hear rumor that he has always wanted to make a picture of this story. Dorian has already been selected an unknown. I read the script some time ago then I got a copy of the book at a second hand store and read it. It had been so many years since I read the book that I couldn't tell how nearly the script followed the book. It differs from the book in omitting entirely the unhealthy homosexual relationship between the artist who painted the portrait and Dorian. I don't know why that is omitted—as that is the important thing the book is about—unless it is too hot a subject to handle from the point of view of the Hays office or something. Oscar Wilde took such pains to write a powerful account of the disintegration of a human soul which had lost its own balance in fastening itself upon the image of Dorian's beautiful face—and never could get itself back together again. The painter's talent was stimulated for a brief moment, then fizzled out and never returned. In making his account one of the workings of the human spirit and one that started in an apparently innocent and high-minded way, he showed even more clearly than if he had made it an ordinary homosexual love affair of the body that this danger is ever present for every human being, and who has to guide his own body and soul in a self-reliant manner, and be ever careful of leaning over much for support in others.*
>
> *"The German woman who wrote* Madchen in Uniform, *a motion picture some years back used this same them of spiritual homosexuality. She wanted to show how dangerous it is in girls' schools, and how innocently innocent ones can fall into it before realizing what is happening to them. Somehow, with delicacy and finesse, a fine motion picture was made of the story without offending anyone. But, evidently this important theme of our time is to be ignored in our version of* Dorian Gray
>
> *The theme that is being played up strongly is the Faust theme Dorian selling his soul to the Devil for eternal youth. Lord Henry Wooton corresponds to Mephistopheles, and uses all the blandishment of flattery and bright talk together with all kinds of arguments from the philosophy of the Cynics and Hedonists. Of course I have always had a quarrel with Oscar Wilde for making Dorian into a romantic character. I think he made his book a dangerous instrument for other naive, untouched but credulous youth in creating this creature of sin and depravity as a beautiful romantic figure. It remains to be seen whether the movie will do the same. Romantic gansters, in one period, set all little boys to copy them. And I suspect that more than one has admired Dorian for Wilde's efforts so I hope that the movie, in showing what not to do—doesn't put too many mischievous ideas into little boy's minds. While I was at the second-hand book store I bought a copy of Marcus Aurelius—his philosophy. I had always wanted a copy so I could read all he had to say—and he is wonderful. Takes the taste of Dorian Gray and Lord Henry's cynic talk out of my mind."*[29]

For Dorian Gray's own house, she fashioned an impressive and fanciful version of the Regency mode which was the popular sophisticated architectural style in London during those years when the story took place. To a considerable degree the Regency style was a style characterized by refined surfaces in highly contrasting dark and light colors. Thus, the black and white film used in the production of Dorian Gray served the architecture very well. The tour-de-force of her design was the three-story stair hall of Dorian Gray's own house. Here she certainly captured the spirit of light and vertical space that one associates with the work of the preeminent Regency architect, Sir John Soane.

Other film sets that she worked on during these years of the Second World War were *The White Cliffs of Dover,* and *Quo Vadis.*[30] For *White Cliffs* she designed the gardens, and a number of the interiors, including John's Bed Room, which was to be *". . . a vigorous Georgian ideal room."*[31] For *Quo Vadis* she noted that *"Bill* [Horning] *is in a rush to get started on* Quo Vadis*—a large Forum scene which he has designed roughly—I am to put it together and make suggested his suggested changes tomorrow."*[32] *Figs. 65, 66, 67*

In her later comments about her experience as a set designer, she remarked that she felt uncomfortable in designing for the unreal world of the film, but nonetheless, many of her designs turned out to be impressive pieces of architecture.

(Fig.69) Woodblock print, "God Bless Us Every One," Christmas/New Year card, 1947.

IV. The Post WWII Modernist Architectural Scene

When looking back into the history of architecture, it is not always easy to recapture the intensity of the emotional as well as intellectual force of the conventions of an era. A case in point would be the emergence of modernism after 1945. While indeed most builder-constructed single family housing during the years 1945 through the late 1950s was still based upon traditional images, plan and site orientation, this was certainly not the case for most architect-designed housing. In writing on the subject of postwar architecture on the West Coast in the London publication, *The Architect's Yearbook,* Walter Landor observed in 1949 that "Modern architecture has reached maturity in the West . . . Modern architects have become socially acceptable, authoritative, and completely 'sound'."[1] He went on to observe that "the architect's brains and souls [had] been purified by the preaching and sometimes the practice of the International Style . . ."[2] *Fig. 68*

The absolute necessity of adopting the modernist credo, and its accepted range of images, emerged in these years with the intensity of a religious belief. There were believers who knew the truth, and then there were a few wayward architects who obviously were lost in sin. The intensity of conflicting truths embroiled in the Cold War scene of these years was matched in the realm of architecture. The modernist "party line," espoused by the taste-maker of the American scene, New York's Museum of Modern Art, and almost universally by the architectural press and the (converted) schools of architecture across the country, revealed not the triumph of a new social and aesthetic order, but of a new religious revelation. Exhibitions and their accompanying publications of the Museum of Modern Art, such as the 1944 "Built in USA: 1932–1944," or the 1952 "Built in USA: Post War Architecture," indicated to architects and others what the modern was about, and what diversity would be tolerated.[3]

With the fewest of exceptions, the older established architects on the American scene, individuals who had generally been trained within the Beaux Art system, were (if not emotionally and intellectually) converted to the modern. Most of these older practitioners approached the world of modern architecture in the same way that they had utilized traditional images, or the popular modernist images of the Art Deco and the Streamline Moderne. *Fig. 69*

The modern, for them, was another style, a new fashion. As products of the Beaux Arts, they did not as a rule simply take over the stylistic elements of the modern; rather, they generally looked to the plan as the generator of a design. Thus, the modernist ideals of the open plan, the breakdown of the separation of indoor and exterior space, the orientation of a house to enclosed gardens and courtyards, etc.

occurred in their postwar designs. With their traditionalist background, the older generation of architects tended to express not surprisingly in their modernist houses more of a concern for the actuality of function, rather than the symbol of the functional (particularly the image of the machine).

With the notable exception of the Miesian International Style Modern advocated in the Case Study House program of John Entenza and his magazine *Arts and Architecture,* most of postwar modernist architects on the West Coast were not doctrinaire in the use of forms. Rather they showed a ". . . preference for the easy, casual warm; intimate integration of house and site; closest possible indoor-outdoor relationship; informality of plan; exposed use of natural materials . . ."[4] Wayne Andrews, in his 1955 *Architecture, Ambition and Americans,* labeled this warm modernism as "Jacobite."[5] He contrasted the warm pragmatic nature of the work of the Jacobites with the cool, impersonal Modern of the "Veblenites."

In Southern California, the principal architects and architectural firms had of course been absorbing modernist elements from the late 1920s on. After World War II, almost all of the architects produced "Jacobite" modernist buildings. This was the case with Paul R. Williams, H. Roy Kelley, Roland E. Coate, Gordon Kaufmann and others. Designers like Cliff May maneuvered the traditional California ranch house into something almost approaching a machine produced product.[6]

Though Riggs continued immediately after the war to produce some traditionalist designs (like the two Colonial/Regency houses, for Parrot at Carmel, 1947), she also turned to the "Jacobite" version of modernism. Upon returning to Santa Barbara from her experience as a film set designer for MGM, she was determined not only to resume her architectural practice, but to carry out her practice in a fashion which was more feasible than had been the case in the late 1930s. She decided to take on a young partner who could help her not only to deal with the new imagery of the modern, but even more important could bring an order and a reality into how she operated as an architect. Her choice fell on the young Pasadena architect, Arvin B. Shaw III. Shaw, who was an avid modernist, had been educated in architecture before the war at Yale, and had worked in the New York office of Wallace K. Harrison (Harrison and Abramovitz).[7] Shaw's own work, such as his two beach houses on Long Island (1958) are purist modern designs, reminiscent of Marcel Breuer and others.[8]

Fig. 70

The partnership of Riggs and Shaw began in 1945 and lasted through 1951. Projects produced during this partnership bore the title of Lutah Maria Riggs, Architect; Arvin B. Shaw III, Office Director. In some projects, such as the 1949–51 Alice Erving house in Montecito, Shaw took the lead, in others Riggs was the prime designer. But no matter who took the lead, it is quite obvious that the final design strongly reflected Riggs's predilections.

The six years from 1945 through 1951 were busy ones. In 1945, there were 16 projects; in 1946, there were 20; and in 1951, there were 16. A number of these were remodelings. Some were not realized, but still a good number proceeded through working drawings and were built. While there were still a few projects outside of Santa Barbara County, most of Riggs's work was right at home so that she did not have to engage in the tiresome travel back and forth to Los Angeles which had taken up so much of her time in the 1930s.

To accommodate her larger practice, Riggs converted her 1926 garage into a drafting studio; and moving into the 1940s added a then-popular open carport (1946) to the side. Her long time friend Miriam Davis moved into the guest quarters of her house, and became the office manager, particularly relieving Riggs of having to take care of the financial records and paying the bills. In the press of producing drawings, two Santa Barbara architects, Glenn Mosher and Richard H. Pitman, helped out on several projects in 1948, and that year Richard B. Nelson joined the office.[9] The drawings from the office indicate that most of the initial sketch plans were drawn by Riggs, some by Shaw. The working drawings were generally produced by others. While a few presentation drawings were produced (by both Riggs and Shaw), there was less of a tendency to produce them when compared to the past. The quality of Lutah's drawings after 1945 does not in any way match her pre-War work. Whether this was due to the association in her mind of fine drawings with her premodernist designs (based upon her Beaux Arts training) or whether she was simply losing her touch is difficult to say.

In her method of design in the thirties, Lutah had frequently produced study models for her designs. For the Kent Parrot House of 1937 in Montecito, she built a cardboard model with the fenestration inked and penciled onto the surfaces. As one would expect, her model for the 1937–38 von Romberg House hovered somewhere between being a study model and a presentation model. After the War she and Shaw quite often had presentation models constructed in the office. These models of the late forties and fifties tended to take the place of perspective drawings and were generally used to present the design to the client.

Most of the d esigns which came from her office during the years 1945 on through the 1950s easily fall within what Walter Landor had in 1949 called, "The California Style," and earlier in 1947, Lewis Mumford had suggested the term, "Bay Tradition," to describe the northern California version of this regionalist tradition.[10] The Southern California version of this informal woodsy tradition was demonstrated in project housing by A. Quincy Jones and Frederick E. Emmons, by Whitney R. Smith and Wayne Williams, by Cliff May and others.[11] *Fig. 76*

Some of the schemes for dwellings from the Riggs office were dominated by a low, pitched gable roofs (with an interior open beam ceiling). Off these were usually projected low flat roof pavilions. A few of the designs were entirely flat roofed with post and lintel construction; a few exhibited single slope shed roofs, or in a few instances, upward-projecting, triangular roofs, such as one finds in the Alice Erving House. Exterior and interior wall surfaces tended to be board and batten or plaster and stucco. Glass was extensively used, and it was usually fenestrated within a repeated pattern of vertical and horizontal structural members. The interiors were generally restrained and somewhat formal, which made it possible to respond to these spaces as being both modern and traditional.

Representative of many of Riggs's houses of the late forties and fifties is the 1947–48 Cotton House in Montecito. Here we discover a characteristic theme of so much of her work, an open recognizable play between traditionalism and modernism. The low-pitched, hipped roof, and informal massing of this house certainly suggest the image of the Colonialized California Ranch house. But the module post and beam grid of its entrance deck and porch, with panels of louvers injected in the walls and in portions of the ceiling, is a pure modernist episode. The garden elevation, however, with its *Fig. 75* central projecting porch, and the interior are formal in character via their symmetry, balance, details and surface materials. Her interest in combining elements of West Coast regionalism, of formalism and of the modern is close to that being pursued by other California architects, particularly William W. Wurster, Gardner Dailey and Joseph Esherick in the Bay Region to the north.[12]

In her use of wood sheathing and above all of exposed wood structure, many of Lutah's post-1945 houses convey an atmosphere shared with the traditional wood houses of Japan. The Leslie Kiler House, sited on a high ridge overlooking Santa Barbara (1955), could easily be mistaken for one of the many northern California houses designed during these years by Wurster, Dailey or Esherick.[13] The play of the low-pitched gable roof which hovers over the flat-roofed porches and the fenestration of thin posts with intervening glass exhibit some of the delicacy of form and detailing of a classic Japanese pavilion.

Another modernist element which Riggs employed was the H-plan, with center of the H being the entrance, with a public zone of living and dining, with their service to one side, and a private section composed of bedrooms and their service areas within the opposite leg of the H. The H-plan was popularized by Marcel Breuer, Hugh Stubbins and others during the years 1945 through the early 1960s, and it was extensively employed by modernist architects across the country. Riggs used this

Fig. 83

scheme, for example, in the Hamilton House (Montecito, 1951). Generally, as in the Hamilton House, she would have the center entrance section read in a formal and symmetrical manner. Then the wings to each side would revert to an informal layout, reflecting their different needs. In these H-plan houses, and others, she varied the ceiling height primarily to retain classic proportions of the interior spaces. The descending order would be for the highest spaces to be the most public, and then she worked down to the lowest ceilings and roofs over service areas.

When *Sunset* magazine presented her 1948 Cooke House in Montecito the editors

Fig. 77

". . . tabulated the reasons why the house was liked and energetically endorsed. (1) It is beautiful in an unostentatious way. (2) It's reserved . . . restrained . . . calm . . . quiet. (3) The plan is uncluttered. (4) Outside and in, it has great livability. (5) It has the mood of a country house . . . relaxed . . . warm . . . colorful . . . comfortable."[14]

In plan the Cooke house carries on the informal layout associated with the pre and postwar California ranch house. Off the central living-dining room with its gabled open beamed ceiling were two angled wings, and then a third wing to the rear. The external and interior detailing of the house nudge it into the modern: clipped eaves, repeated floor to ceiling glass openings, and the combined horizontal porch and pergola on the garden side supported by metal pipe columns. At the entrance side of the house the modernist theme of horizontality is established via the pipe-supported porch roof which continues to one side to become the flat roof of the carport.

Of the houses designed during the Riggs and Shaw partnership, the most doctrinaire modern was the small Gross Beach House at Sandyland Cove (1949).[15] The

Fig. 79

intent of this design was to suggest a stucco box with its extended, parapeted deck suspended over the sandy beach. To create this illusion, the lower floor is recessed inward and is sheathed in dark redwood board and batten. The open plan of the house and details such as the corner floor to glass walls which flow into the large stone fireplace have a strong similarity to the post-World War houses of Richard J. Neutra. Nevertheless, in contrast with the designs of Neutra, the interior of the Gross House in its exposed beam ceilings and its grayed birch plywood walls conveyed an informal, non-insistent modernist quality. The editors of *Sunset* noted in this regard, "Their (the architects) refusal to follow any style down the line gives the house a casual quality a comfort, that is inviting and real."[16]

A play between the old and new was carried out in the small Robert Mazet House (1950) in Montecito. Here Riggs and Shaw reverted to an old structural/aesthetic device of revealing the actual frame on the exterior. The frame itself was of 3 inch by 4 inch posts, with an infill of ¾ inch waterproof plywood. The project consisted of a small weekend dwelling and a separate carport with an attached guest suite. The Mazet house was unquestionably meant to be viewed as modern with its flat roof and a careful infill of fixed and moveable glass units. Similar exposed frame, modular dwellings had been produced by America's contingent of modernists from the early 1930s on (in California one thinks of modernist houses of the thirties designed by R. M. Schindler, Richard J. Neutra, Gregory Ain and others). As Riggs remarked in the mid-1960s, the idea of using the exposed frame as the dominant theme of the building was a good one, but from her experience it always turned out to be expensive to build, and generally expensive to maintain.[17]

Of the designs from the Riggs office in the late 1940s there are three which substantially depart from the woodsy modernist norm of the West Coast. These were the projected country house for Burton G. Tremaine, Jr. at Serena Beach, Santa Barbara County (1947), a ranch house near Winslow, Arizona, also for the Tremaine's (1947–48), and the Alice Erving House in Montecito (1949–51). The conceptual design for the Tremaine House at Serena Beach was from the hand of the Brazilian modernist architect, Oscar Niemeyer, with the landscape design by Roberto Burle Marx. In his presentation of the work of Oscar Neimeyer in 1950, Stamo Papadaki wrote of the Tremaine house, "Climatic condition and local exuberance produced the design of this California residence . . ."[18] *Figs. 71, 72*

The task of Riggs and Shaw was to take this scheme and to provide the working drawings and specifications and then to supervise the construction of the house.[19] The center portion of the house was to have been a low horizontal rectangular two-story volume. The enclosed space of the house wandered in and out of the module of steel posts. The rectangular rigidit y of the design was countered by a circular form for the dining room, and then by a curved wandering roof slab which ended up at a pair of dressing rooms for the adjacent pool.

For the Burton Tremaine, Jr. Ranch House, "Meteor-Crater Ranch," near Winslow, Arizona, Riggs and Shaw turned to the geometry of the circle. The livable spaces of the house occupied approximately half of the circle, while three pairs of tack rooms and an open hitching rail closed in the circle. At the center of the open courtyard was a circular swimming pool. A shed roof pitched upward from the exterior of the circle forming a high interior wall which defined a section of the interior courtyard. The low exterior walls of the C-shaped form of the house were of rustic vertical logs, while the high curved wall facing the courtyard exhibited a smooth thin wall sheathed in and broken by three large glass areas. Thus, externally the building resembled a traditional ranch building, while within the courtyard the concentric curved wall and its *Figs. 73, 74* fenestration pointed to the modern.

One would assume that the inspiration for the design of the Tremaine Ranch House was Frank Lloyd Wright's well-publicized second Herbert Jacobs House of 1943 at Middletown, Wisconsin. In Wright's project, the enclosed section of the house occupies a segment of the circle, while the remainder of the circle (a protected courtyard) was established by a raised earth berm. Though the theme of the Tremaine Ranch House goes back to Wright's earlier scheme, the Riggs/Shaw design went off in a different direction by playing an open game between the vernacular rustic and the modern.

While these two exciting Tremaine designs remained as unbuilt projects, their house for Alice Erving was built, and it turned out to be their most publicized design.[20]

On December 2, 1944, Alice Erving had written to Riggs, who was then in Culver City working for MGM, indicating that she and her mother had purchased a site on San Ysidro Road upon which they were planning to build "a small modern house."[21] Alice Erving went on to say that "As you know mother has always admired your work and hoped some day to be able to have you do a house for us. We have been reading up on modern architecture and would like to take advantage of the new techniques and materials and the modern concept of aesthetics. I have just finished reading Giedion's *Space, Time and Architecture* which I found fascinating."[22] Riggs first discussed the project with Alice and her mother during the Christmas holidays of 1944. A variety of circumstances, including the need to sell the family's large Montecito house, prevented the Ervings from commencing the project until 1948.[23]

In writing about the Erving house in 1952, the editors of *House and Home* commented, "For this is, above all, a very poetic house—and regardless of whether or not you like each individual stanza, the architects certainly produced a fine flight of fancy with a lot of common sense . . . This functional house is a good example of how a functional program can be transformed into an exciting poetic piece of architecture."[24] In the early 1960s Alice Erving observed that the concept of the design of the house was by Shaw, and that the poetry and the careful functional detailing of it came from Riggs.[25]

Figs. 80, 81, 82

The house was sited on a slight knoll, within a grove of existing oaks. On this knoll the architects had placed a dramatic prismatic triangle, whose high apex with its glass infill wall captured a theatrical view of the Santa Ynez Mountains to the north. The two lower sides of the triangle faced towards the southeast and southwest, and they captured a distant view of the Pacific Ocean. The triangular space was divided into three spaces by a large stone fireplace and chimney mass and by a low storage unit (which reached up only part way). To the north was an entrance and long lanai, to the southeast was the living room which worked itself around the fireplace mass to the dining room. Two wings project off this high triangular space: the kitchen and guest bedroom to the west and the master bedroom, bath and a photographic dark room to the east.

To the north of the glass-walled lanai was the carport. The south wall of the carport, plus a wall to the west, transformed this space into a partially enclosed patio. The approach to the house was down the west side of the carport and then under a flat roof which was suspended and cantilevered from beams. Working closely with the San Francisco landscape architect, Thomas Church, the Riggs office provided an extensive series of wide wooden decks located off the southwest facing dining room. With the exception of the auto court and the north patio, Church designed the landscape so that the viewer would see the garden as being natural to the site.[26]

If we think in terms of what was being designed during these years, it is obvious that the dramatic form of the Alice Erving House reflects Shaw's (and to a degree Riggs's as well) interest in the work of other modernist of the time, especially the work of Eliel and Eero Saarinen. In its approach to geometric forms, structure and suspended roof systems, the Saarinen's 1944 design for the Tanglewood Opera House (Lenox, Massachusetts) shared a number of qualities with the Alice Erving House.[27] But not only did the designs of both the Tremaine Ranch House and the Alice Erving House share qualities with several of America's modernists of the late forties, the Riggs designs also anticipated the fascination with the use of "pure" geometric forms which appreciably expanded within American architecture of the 1950s.

(Fig. 91) Garden for Daniel J. Donohue house "Villa San Giuseppe,"Los Angeles, 1956-67. (Photo: Marvin Rand)

V. The 1960s & 70s, a Resurgence of Traditionalism

RIGGS CONTINUED, IN THE YEARS AFTER 1945, TO BE INVOLVED WITH THE LOCAL and national affairs of the A.I.A., being President once again of the local Chapter (1953) and serving on the National Committee on Preservation of Historic Buildings (1955). From 1955 on through the 1960s, she was Preservation Officer of the local Chapter of the A.I.A. In 1960, she was made a Fellow of the A.I.A.

In the 1920s and 1930s, she had assisted Pearl Chase (Santa Barbara's most influential advocate of planning and of architectural controls, from the early 1920s on through the early 1970s), and the Santa Barbara Plans and Planting Committee on numerous projects. In the late fifties and on through the early seventies, she became even more involved with the formation in the early 1960s of the City and the County General plans. The group most instrumental in initiating the General Plans for the county and the city was the Citizens Planning Association of Santa Barbara County, Inc. This association was formed in 1960, and Riggs was one of its founding members. She remained on its Board of Directors through the late 1960s. Pearl Chase also prevailed upon her to turn more of her attention to historic preservation within the City of Santa Barbara, within Montecito, and in the county at large. She served from 1960 on the County Historic Preservation Commission, and she was a founding member of the city's Advisory Landmark Committee.

On the state level she served from 1961 through 1964 as a member of the State Board of Architectural Examiners. Clark Kerr, then president of the University of California, appointed her in 1958 to the Professional Advisory Council to the School of Architecture at Berkeley. Along with Pietro Belluschi, Gardner Dailey, Frank Kent and Stephen C. Pepper (with William W. Wurster as the architectural adviser), she was appointed in 1961 as a juror for the Competition for a new Governor's Mansion for California.[1] The winning design for this unbuilt project was won by the San Francisco firm of Campbell and Wong. Their design, which took into account both the current rage for the Classical Decorated Pavilion, as well as California's 19th-century Monterey tradition, certainly reflected Riggs's view at that moment of what would be appropriate as a symbolic image for California.[2]

In the mid-forties Riggs again found herself involved with the designing of stage sets. In 1946 she did the set for Ferenc Molnar's *The Guardsman.* The following year she designed the set for a local production at the Lobero Theater of Paul Vincent Carroll's *Shadow and Substance.* Both of these designs evoked an "Old English" feeling. The center of attention of the principal set for *Shadow and Substance* was a stone wall pierced by a wide Gothic tracery window.

Riggs's activities with the profession took her frequently to Sacramento and to

Washington, D.C. While these trips were often stimulating, they were hardly relaxing. In 1949, with Shaw running the office, she felt she could leave and take a trip for pleasure, and as she put it "to see and to learn."[3] The February trip on the Dutch liner "Nieuw Amsterdam" included visits to Cuba, a number of the other islands and to Panama. Her letters and photographs indicated that she searched out the older traditional one- and two-story houses, and she made a point of visiting many of the new postwar modernist buildings.

After Shaw returned to New York to work permanently for Wallace Harrison, Riggs's office remained small, usually consisting of two to three draftspersons. For a brief period in 1964, there was a "trial partnership" with Richard B. Nelson, who had first entered the office in 1948. This partnership was dissolved after a few months. Others entered the office, some very briefly, like Paul Tuttle, others for longer periods of time, like David Smith. In the late 1960s, Riggs was assisted by R. Deming Isaacson, a graduate of the architectural program at Yale, and by Joseph Knowles (who entered her office in 1964), a Stanford graduate, who remained with her until her office was closed in the late 1970s.[4]

Riggs's designs of the three decades of the 1950s through the 1970s reflect a major shift which took place across the country. With only a few exceptions, her work of the fifties continued her commitment to modernism, albeit of a Jacobite rather than a Veblenite character. After 1960, on the other hand, many of her most important designs signal a return to traditionalist architectural images. While many of these late designs share a recourse to traditionalism with the post-1965 exponents of post modernism, it should be noted that her designs are not postmodernist in intent. In contrast to the postmodernist who employed historic (almost always derived from the Classical traditions) images as comments on the past, Riggs and other older practitioners approached these images as vital and alive links between the past and the present; simply a continuation of their Period Revival designs of the earlier years).

Figs. 89, 100, 101

Riggs's modernist work of the 1950s and early 1960s wavered between the modernized California ranch house to the structurally declared post and beam aesthetic. This grid aesthetic was, of course, a dominant one in much of the modernist architecture of California in the 1950s as well as in the 1960s. The post and beam aesthetic was, of course, the theme of the Case Study House program of *Arts and Architecture*. This design approach was closely associated with the architectural program of the University of Southern California.

Figs. 94, 95, 96

An example of the latter was the C. Pardee Erdman House (Montecito, 1957–59).[5] The plan of the Erdman house is in the form of a U, which centers on a axially oriented swimming pool. To the east a formal entrance platform defined by corner piers faces out to the auto court. Having made a formal statement by the symmetrical platform and the wide set of double doors leading into the entrance gallery, Riggs suggests the informal and utilitarian via the carports which adjoin the entrance platform. While fragments of the plan and certain of the elevations are formal in character, the overall plan appears as an informal response to functional needs. The general atmosphere of the Erdman house is that of a light classical pavilion, similar in spirit to the concurrent work on the national scene of Edward D. Stone or of several of the late Case Study House projects of Killingsworth, Brady and Associates.[6]

Of her more traditionalist designs, the extensive remodeling of J. James and Elizabeth Hollister House (1953) and of the A.C. Pedotti House (1956), both in Santa Barbara, illustrated her continued fondness for California's Hispanic tradition. In this instance, she showed her abilities of being able to be a traditionalist and a modernist in the way she united two older Spanish Colonial Revival buildings. "Both new and remodeled portions of this house in Santa Barbara, California, faithfully follow the old Spanish style of the original structures," wrote the editors of *Sunset*.[7] The magazine editors observed how Riggs successfully played off the theme of modernity with a "... clean, almost contemporary interior. . . ," which at the same time was "... reminiscent of the white-washed Spanish ranch house . . ."[8] *Figs. 78, 90*

One of Riggs's principal patrons of the postwar years was the art collector, Wright Ludington. In 1952, she had remodeled Wright's Mediterranean villa on Sycamore Canyon (the former Dater House, designed in 1916 by Bertram G. Goodhue). In the mid-fifties Ludington had purchased a large mountainside site in eastern Montecito. Upon this Riggs was commissioned to build a villa, "Hesperides" which would convey a sense of tradition as well as modernity. The design for this house looks back directly to the abstracted traditionalism of the 1937–38 von Romberg house.

The main house is contained within two overlapping white stucco volumes. The traditional aspect of these two boxes is revealed in their classic, almost Palladian-like proportions, in their finely detailed cornice, and in sparsely occurring windows and doors. A suggestion of hierarch y is alluded to via the size and detailing of the various box-like enclosures. The highest volume is that of the double cube living room; the next lower volume contained the picture gallery entrance and other rooms; while to each side of the entrance motor court are secondary buildings housing guest quarters, garages, and such. *Figs. 97, 98, 99*

The principal doors and windows were symmetrically placed within their respective wall surfaces. Thus, the entrance door established the central axis of the auto court; while the high-roofed loggia of the south garden facade serves as the starting point for an axis which runs through the long swimming pool and through the center of the ocean viewing pillared pavilion. The thin elongated proportions of the detailing of the south garden side of the house and its outbuilding seems to hint at the delicacy of a 17th or 18th century Persian (Iranian) garden pavilion. The gardens, designed by Elizabeth de Forest, together with classical sculpture, columns and architectural fragments were meant to draw one into the atmosphere of Classical Rome and the Mediterranean coast.

The west entrance off the auto court lead one directly into the picture gallery, a tall axial space, with walls which were almost black. With the paintings artificially lighted, the effect was that of rich, brilliant series of jewels suspended in a mysterious dark open space. In the center of the gallery's long south wall were double doors which lead into the great living room. The proportions of the living room were that of a pair of Palladio's cubes. In contrast, the remainder of the house was far more informal, and the guest wing (which also contain the changing rooms for the pool) seemed almost rural and rustic.

In the early 1970s Ludington decided to build yet another country house, one which would be smaller and less demanding of his attention. The site in this case was a low ridge in the eastern Montecito valley which enjoyed a sweeping view of the ocean, both to the south and to the southeast. This house, "October Hill," (1972–73) went *Figs. 103, 104, 105* through an abstracting process similar to that of the earlier house. Only here, the traditionalism which was abstracted was that of a Mexican or Spanish hacienda. The use of a rural "primitive" architectural source places the design squarely within the style of Smith's work of the 1920s. The broad unbroken white walls of the house suggest the "Cubist" houses of a Cezanne painting. Historical architectural remembrances are once again limited: the parapet terminated by the subtle shadow line of a cornice, windows and doors articulated by heavy wood louver shutters, and finally a sparse use of projecting canales (roof drains). Again, as in the earlier Ludington House, the garden and the house are integral. Running parallel to the south front of the house are terraced masonry platforms, and pools. These terminate, to the east, in a composition of four white piers which have a suggestion of the ruins of a classical temple. The gardens were designed by Wright and Elizabeth de Forest.

Two of Riggs's other major commissions of the late 1950s were the remodeling of El Paseo and the design of the exterior of the adjoining Suski building (1964–65) in Santa Barbara, and the development of the gardens of "Villa San Giuseppe" (1956–65) in Los Angeles. Together with Santa Barbara's early 19th century Mission Church, the late 1920s Santa Barbara County Courthouse and the Fox Arlington Theater, the El Paseo complex has been, since it was completed in 1923, one of the city's principal architectural landmarks. The complex consisted of the famed nineteenth-century De La Guerra Adobe which was interwoven into one of the West Coast's first pedestrian shopping centers by the architect James Osborn Craig.[9]

At the center of the complex was a courtyard and an open patio restaurant. These were connected to the three adjoining streets by romantic paseos, the most important one being the Street of Spain which led off De La Guerra Street. The Suski's as the new owners, felt that some changes were needed to make the complex economically feasible. One of these was to open the complex up in a more formal fashion to State Street. The other was to increase the density of use by building a new five-story office building adjacent and to the north of the complex. Riggs was engaged to provide the new State Street entrance and to renovate other portions of the complex. She struggled for well over a year with the design for the State Street Paseo entrance, but it never seemed fully to come together. Though it provided the new openness which the client wished for, she felt that she was never able to capture, as she put it, the "charm" of the earlier work.[10]

Fig. 102

Her exterior design for the Suski Building was in many ways a more complex and difficult problem, yet the results were far more satisfactory. The building itself, designed by Victor Gruen Associates of Los Angeles, was a slab, five stories in height. Riggs was brought in at the last moment to provide a design which would read as a traditional Mediterranean/Hispanic building which would complement the adjoining El Paseo complex. Despite the numerous limitations placed on her—the height of the structure, its established shape, and the budgetary limitations—her accomplishment was impressive. Via the use of a series of horizontal false cornices she projected the sense of a traditional layered building. The window surrounds were slightly projected forward which enhanced the masonry feeling of the structure. She used hipped tile roofs at the east and west ends of the building and for the sixth floor service area. She treated the two ends of the building as pavilions, and then she articulated the space between as three floors of loggias. She placed great emphasis on traditional detailing, especially in the iron work and in the cast stone. Though the building is too close and is out of scale with the adjacent El Paseo complex, its design is contextual and does not clash with the Andalusian forms of Craig's original architecture.

As far as the general public and the architectural profession is concerned, Rigg's most widely known and admired work has been the Vedanta Temple in eastern Montecito (1954-56).[11] The renown of the Temple within her practice matches the success of Lloyd Wright in his 1949 Wayfarer's Chapel at Palos Verdes. Both of these religious structures are impressive as designs, both are dramatically situated with views looking over the Pacific (and in the case of the Vedanta Temple, with a view to the Santa Ynez Mountains as well). Finally, both of these designs are as much in the realm of landscape architecture as in architecture itself.

Figs. 84, 85, 86, 87, 88

In Riggs's case, her ability to arrive at a design which took the viewer in two directions—traditionalism and modernism—was a direct result of her Beaux Arts training. She related in later years that at the time she had no real knowledge of Chinese and Japanese architecture, other than the usual casual interest which most West Coast designers have had. She plunged into books and articles on the subject ranging from such early classics as Edward S. Morse's 1886 *Japanese Houses and Their Surroundings* and Ralph Adams Cram's 1905 *Impressions of Japanese Architecture* to more recent volumes on Japanese and Chinese architecture and landscape architecture.[12]

The gabled, sweeping roofed temple was placed on a low-raised platform and was approached from the south by a bank of stairs. The tiled roof was projected far out from the walls and was supported by paired rafters. The vertical log posts supported the exposed lintel and roof were left partially exposed within the white plastered wall surfaces. This rhythmic effect encourages one to respond to the building as being derived from traditionalist concepts, as well as those of the modernist. As with her earlier Hispanic designs and with her postwar modernist design, Riggs looked to the theme of carefully thought out simplicity to create an abstracted version of a traditional form.

In 1958 Riggs began on her most extensive commission of these years, the garden of the Daniel J. Donohue house in the Los Feliz district of Los Angeles. Once again, this time in her Studebaker Lark convertible (later in her Mercedes), she commuted back and forth between Santa Barbara and Los Angeles. This Medieval image (more French than English) house had been designed for the exuberant Los Angeles radio station owner and Packard dealer, Earle C. Anthony.[13] It was designed in 1924–26 by Bernard Maybeck of Berkeley, who had designed several of Anthony's Packard dealership buildings in northern and southern California.[14] The gifted planner, landscape architect, and architect Mark Daniels had designed the gardens of the eight-acre estate.[15] As happened in a number of instances in Southern California, work on the garden began in 1923, so that when the house was finished in 1926 there would be at least a partially established garden.

Figs. 91, 92, 93

Daniels re-contoured and planted the greater part of hilltop site so that it would appear natural in the fashion of a late 18th century English Picturesque garden. Up close to the house he introduced several formal Italian elements. "Happily," he wrote, "the general parti is non-symmetrical. On the major axis, which passes through the formal gardens, the arched windows of the dining room and drawing room face one another over a pool of cerulean blue. Opposite to each other on the minor axis running through this pool, are the studios and living quarters."[16] The main formal feature of Daniel's scheme was an axial garden which extended off the principal axis of the Drawing Room. Retaining walls topped by stone balustrades contained this long narrow platform garden. The end of the axis embraced ". . . a view of distant city and mountains that cannot be surpassed from any terrace on the slopes of Fiesole."[17]

The interest of the Donohues was to enlarge and to expand the gardens of the estate to provide a new, more formal entrance and then to accentuate even more the illusion of a late medieval Italian country villa situated within a High Renaissance garden. With this in mind they engaged the highly respected Los Angeles landscape architect Howard Sadler, but he passed away suddenly. They then went to A.E. Hanson, who had completed Mrs. Donohue's mother (Mrs. Daniel Murphy) garden on Adams Boulevard in the early 1930s. He did not feel that he could take on the task, and he recommended Riggs (who was known to Mrs. Donohue, since she had worked with Hanson on the Murphy garden). Riggs was engaged to carry on with the garden, and she continued to work on it through 1968 when Mrs. Donohue died.

As already mentioned the one strong formal features of the garden dating back to the Anthonys was the northeast terrace which extended off the drawing room loggia and the internal court with its oval swimming pool. By the late 1950s, Riggs had added new high walls which faced onto the adjoining streets. A new more grand entrance gateway was provided, and off this was a new roadway which gradually wound its way up the hillside. To make this road possible she added high masonry retaining walls both above and below the roadway. The new roadway terminated at a second set of gates, which led into a circular court. Off this court, on axis, was the final drive which led up to the entrance and the auto court and to the other side was an open classical pavilion. A third set of low gateposts marked the division between the round court and the drive as it lead to the auto court. At the Medieval entrance (with tower and portcullis) to the house, Riggs designed a new set of formal stairs, and, opposite these stairs and the auto court, she provided a newly added axis which led down through a series of walled, formally planted gardens. All of the new walls, balustrades and other features were carried out in reinforced concrete, cast stone and some cut stone. Historic garden pavilions and statuary were placed on the northeast terrace, at the circular entrance to the upper drive, and within the new terraced gardens to the southeast of the new entrance and auto court.

Riggs's designs (working closely with the Donohues) for the gardens and the grounds of the estate were Italian based upon late 15th and early 16th century examples from Tuscany. The most memorable feature of the garden was the northeast terrace. Riggs extended the earlier platform garden, lowered a portion of it, and introduced a strong pattern of different colored stones. She eliminated the Daniels' smaller central pool, and at the far end of the platform, she placed a grand tiered fountain. The sides of the patterned stone surface were defined by long continuous rows of potted plants, back of which were a row of trees (one row to each side) which were precisely clipped into two continuous rectangular bands of greenery. Paved walks to each side paralleled the balustrades which had been part of the original design. The most romantic feature of the gardens, which matches the romance of

Maybeck's design for the house, is the circular northeast driveway entrance. Here a small circular, open domed classical pavilion (brought from Europe by the Donohues) was framed by trees through which one gets a glimpse of the distant San Gabriel Mountains. The scene is highly reminiscent of the turn of the century illustrations of Maxfield Parrish, especially those made for Edith Wharton's influential volume, *Italian Villas and Their Gardens*.[18] Since Maybeck himself had created a country house which suggested that it had accumulated new additions over many years, Riggs's gardens enhance rather than clash with the house. When completed, one experiences the gardens as if they and the house were designed at the same moment.

In the 1970s there was an increased demand upon the part of her clients to return to traditional images, especially the Spanish Colonial Revival. Examples of this approach are evidenced in her Hispanic designs for the projected Eldon Haskell House (Santa *Fig. 106* Ynez Mountains above Santa Barbara, 1977) and in the last house to come from her office, the Jack C. Antrium House (Goleta, 1978–80).[19] The Haskell scheme was a classic patio-oriented Hispanic design. The slope of the site encouraged different levels, including a bridge-like entrance which lead to the front door. The Antrium *Fig. 107* house, situated on another mountain site, also responded to the change of levels of the site, being two stories in height at the south end and one story at its north or entrance end. The two-story portion to the south was treated with a traditional projecting Monterey porch on its second level.

Thus, by the final decade of her career as an architect, Riggs had returned to the use of historic, regional images which she had been introduced to in the Smith office. As in her earliest work, her aesthetic interest in these late houses was to create structures which by their proportions, careful layout of windows, doors and other elements in relation to the dominant white stucco walls would be recognized within the dualism of traditionalism and modernism.

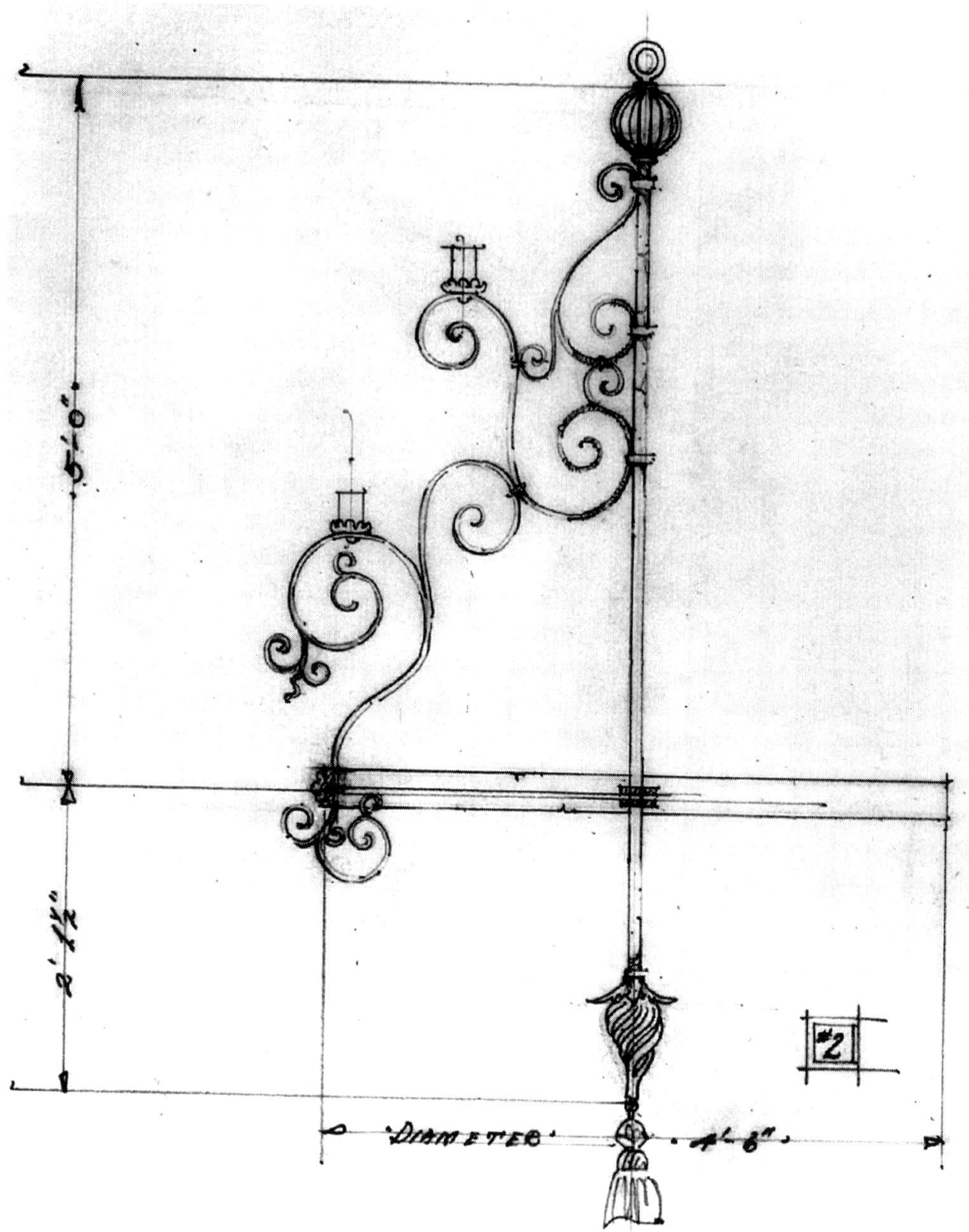

Candelabra for George Cameron's music room.

VI. Lutah Maria Riggs, a Woman in Architecture

In the obituary she wrote in 1930 for George Washington Smith, she characterized him as "*. . . of a retiring nature, modest and reserved, and not adept at small talk.*"[1] Her portrait of Smith as a "retiring" individual fits Riggs with as much accuracy as Smith. She was by her own admission, a "private person," and as inept at "small talk" as her mentor. There were difference to be sure. While "reserved" in general matters, she was sharp, critical and quite vocal in issues which interested her. In public and private, she could and did express her positive and negative views, especially in the realms of architecture and planning. As the strength of her architectural designs indicates, she held certain very strong beliefs and expressed them in her work. With the exception of notes and personal letters, she, like Smith, never wrote about architecture or about planning issues. Her comment, in this regard, was a classic one, namely that the buildings themselves constitute the language of architecture; there was no real need for a designer to turn to the language of the written word to indicate what she or he was about. On the other hand she had always been interested in history, and she not only looked at books and articles on architecture, but she generally read the text as well. In the mid-1960s, she remarked that she found Frank Lloyd Wright far more fascinating as a writer (particularly in his *Autobiography*) than as a designer of buildings.[2]

As her projected and built buildings indicate, Riggs obtained only a few commissions outside of the residential field. There were a number of reasons for this dearth of non-domestic commissions. She carried on the Smith tradition of practicing the profession in the time-honored fashion of the gentlewomen/gentleman architect. The image she and Smith conveyed was not that of the business-person architect, but rather that of an upper-middle-class individual who was an "art architect," to use an old nineteenth-century term. This was reinforced by the location of her practice—not in an office situated in the downtown of a city, but in a studio located in her home. Added to this was the location of her home in an acknowledged residential retreat of the wealthy and upper middle class.

In the early 1930s as she traveled back and forth between Santa Barbara and her work in Los Angeles, she had seriously toyed with the idea of permanently moving her practice to Los Angeles. She was fully aware that even in prosperous times the small enclave of Santa Barbara offered limited possibilities for making a living as an architect. But she really loved Santa Barbara, and it was there that most of her friends lived, and she enjoyed a widespread reputation as an architect. As far as her practice is concerned, there is no question that these potential contacts were real, for once the economy began to burst forth after World War II she enjoyed some 25 years of more commissions than she often could adequately handle.

Riggs did indeed enjoy the respect of several of Santa Barbara's business personages, but she never cultivated the business community for commissions; nor did she seek to indicate that she would be delighted to be considered by political figures, or governmental bureaucrats for public building. For most of the local business people and the political figures, she was thought of as an architect who designed residences for the "Montecito Squiredom." In addition, her public expressed views on local and regional planning issues, her close involvement with Pearl Chase, and the Citizens Planning Association placed her (in their minds) in the wrong camp.

A final issue which must be touched upon has to do with the fact that Riggs was a women involved in what was (and still is) a profession dominated by men. This was an issue which she was all too aware of, but it was one which, within the image of herself as a private person, she seldom wished to discuss. She, on occasion, would remark that she strongly resented the view that since she was a woman she would obviously be able to design a well laid-out kitchen, the specific area of traditional women's work. On the other hand, with the spate of intensified interest in women's ability to participate as equals in society, she felt ill at ease when she was cited as a successful woman in architecture. In the 1970s when her work was often being exhibited nationwide, she felt that instead of being honored she was being "used" by feminists for their own purpose. She felt that the feminists were suggesting that her work should be judged and responded to as the work of a woman when she wished to be judged as an architect.[3]

In 1912, the Editors of the California publication, *Architect and Engineer* commented in an article "The Woman Architect," that "There is no sex to genius . . . women frequently can and would make first-class designers of residences as well as other structures . . ."[4] Though Riggs was quite active in the profession, serving twice as President of the local Chapter of the A.I.A., being made a fellow of the A.I.A., and serving on the State of California Board of Architectural Examiners, she was not mentioned in the two long articles "A Thousand Women in Architecture," published in the *Architectural Record* in 1948.[5]

This lack of recognition was most probably due to the few examples of her designs which were published in national and regional journals (or in the middle and upper middle class home shelter magazines). In looking at her work of the 1930s, designs such as the von Romberg house, the Walker House, or several of her houses within Rolling Hills should have been published, but, as she remarked in later years, she felt that she neither had the time nor the funds needed to publicize her work.

If the work had been submitted, say in the mid to late 1930s, there is no reason to think that it would not have been published. The work of such women architects as Victorine Homsey or of Verna Cook Salamonsky (Shipway) was extensively published in the thirties, and in their use of architectural images ranging from the traditional to the modern, their designs were quite similar to those of Riggs.[6]

Harriet Rochlin in an article published in the August 1977 issue of the *Journal of the American Institute of Architects* states that ". . . an atmosphere of professional hospitality" in California made this region more open for a woman practitioner than other areas of the country.[7] The five architects she cites are Julia Morgan, Hazel Waterman,

Lilian Rice, Edla Muir and Lutah Maria Riggs. Of these, only three—Morgan, Muir and Riggs—really established long and successful practices. As the 1948 article in the *Record* indicates, there were as many successful women architects in the Northeast and Midwest as there were on the West Coast. Perhaps, L.A. and Southern California were more open and "laid-back" in their reception to women architects than other regions of the country, but if so, it was only to a minor degree.

In a brief article, published in the *Southwest Builder and Contractor* for August 14, 1936, the highly successful New York architect Verna Cook Salamonsky wrote, "The reason comparatively few [women] are top-notchers [in architecture] is that it is fearfully hard work. Sometimes you work two or three days or nights without stopping. I think only women with super-vitality can stand it." And this latter characterization certainly applies to Riggs—her pratice was a difficult one to carry out, but she did it.[8]

Responding to Riggs's wish to be judged simply as an architect, there is no question, in the mind of this author, that a number of her designs represent major monuments of twentieth-century American architecture. These are the von Romberg House, the Alice Erving House, the second Wright Ludington House, the Vedanta Temple, and the Donohue Garden. Whatever the imagery might be, her designs conveyed those qualities she most admired, "purity and simplicity," coupled with a sense of "restfulness and peacefulness."[9]

As a product of the Beaux Arts educational system, Riggs approached design through the pl an—both in regard to aesthetic experience and function. Like others who had been trained within this program, she held fast to Classical systems of proportion. She had been firmly taught how to study the languages of style and then how to use these languages in her buildings. As her career indicates, she approached historic form as a source and then sought to make it contemporary.

Her designs of the 1930s illustrate her open reception of the new—ranging from the popular Art Deco and Streamline Moderne to high art International style. After World War II, she fell with ease into the West Coast warm and non-doctrinaire modern. Her final designs from the late 1960s on should be seen as her response not only to the then current fashion of postmodernist, but to the earlier episode of modernism. But these late buildings, as was the case with her earliest work of the mid 1920s, always existed within the visual world of architecture; they were never intellectual comments on architecture.

(Fig. 1) Riggs and fellow women architectural students in front of the "Ark," University of California, Berkeley, 1920. L to r: Margaret Read, Elah Hale, Lutah Maria Riggs, Margaret Monroe.

(Fig. 2) Student ink sketch of the street of a medieval French city, 1918.

(Fig. 4) Student conte crayon figurative drawing "Memory," for architectural sculpture, 1917

(Fig. 3) Student pencil figurative drawing from a bronze sculpture by Mahonni Young, 1918.

(Fig. 6, opposite) Student conte crayon drawing of imaginary country house, 1918.

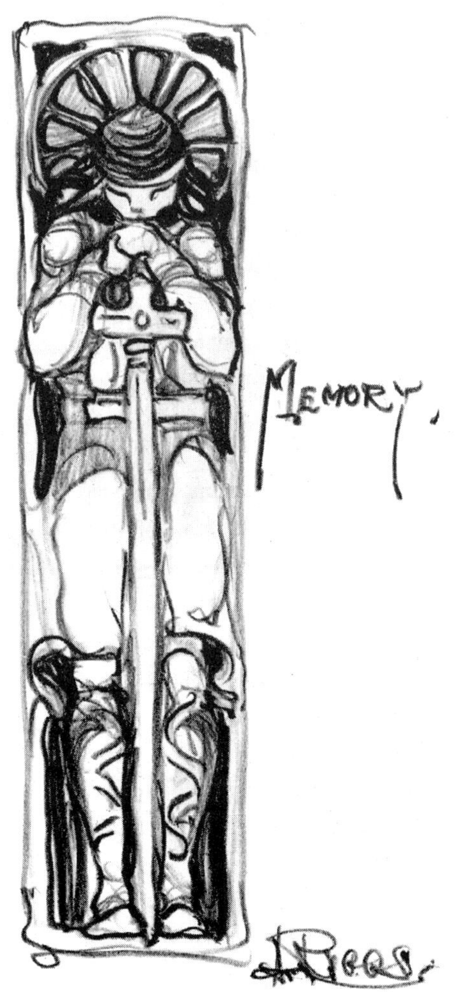

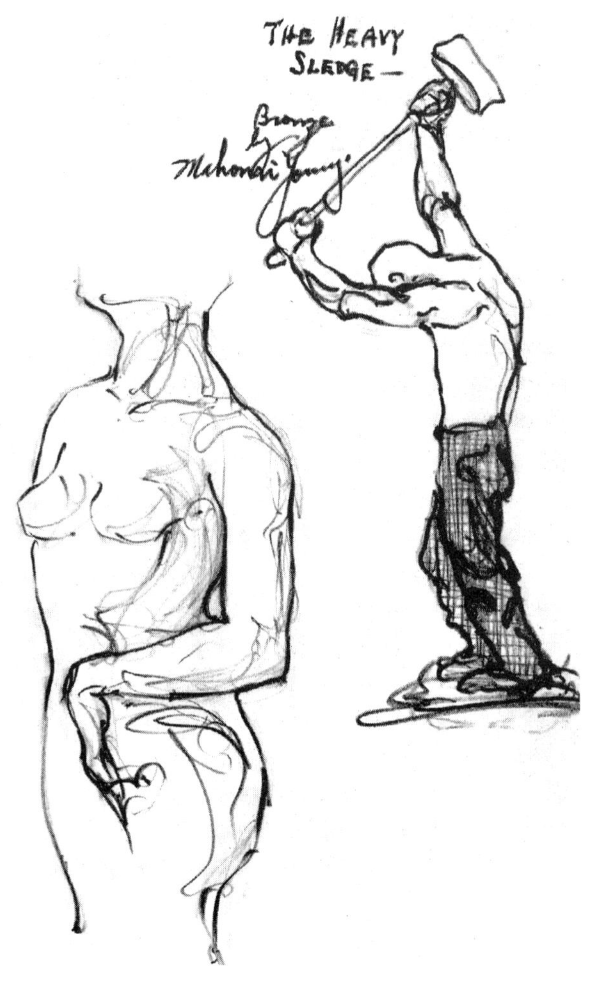

(Fig. 7) Pencil drawing of a rural building near Susanville, 1920.

(Fig. 8) Pencil drawing of a tree near Susanville, 1920.

(Fig. 9) Pencil drawing of the Thayer's Barn, Sonoma County, 1921.

THE THAYERS' BARN -
5-8-21 -

(Fig. 10, 11) Pencil drawing for GWS, "House A," Ojai. 1922.

(Fig. 5) Student watercolor drawing: imaginary scene of the Alhambra in Spain, 1917

(Fig. 5) Student watercolor drawing: imaginary scene of the Alhambra in Spain, 1917.

(Fig. 13) Pencil drawing for GWS for projected book on Mexican architecture, 1923.

(Fig. 14) Conte crayon drawing of "The Early Mass," Pala, Mexico, 1922.

(Fig. 16) Conte drayon drawing of sailboars in Santa Barbara harbor, c. 1922-23.

(Fig. 17,) Conte crayon drawing of Santa Barbara harbor, c. 1922-23.

(Fig. 15, opposite) Ink and conte drayon drawing of "Old House"in Mexico City, 1923.

(Fig. 18) Conte crayon drawing for GWS for "El Mercado de la Fiesta," in De la Guerra Plaza, Santa Barbara, 1927.

THE · DAILY · NEW
·EL·MERCADO·DE·LA·FIESTA·
·SANTA·BARBARA·1927·

(Fig. 19) Pencil drawing for GWS "For Sale sign," c. 1925.

(Fig. 20) Conte crayon drawing for GWS for Fagan/Crocker house, Pebble Beach, 1927-30.

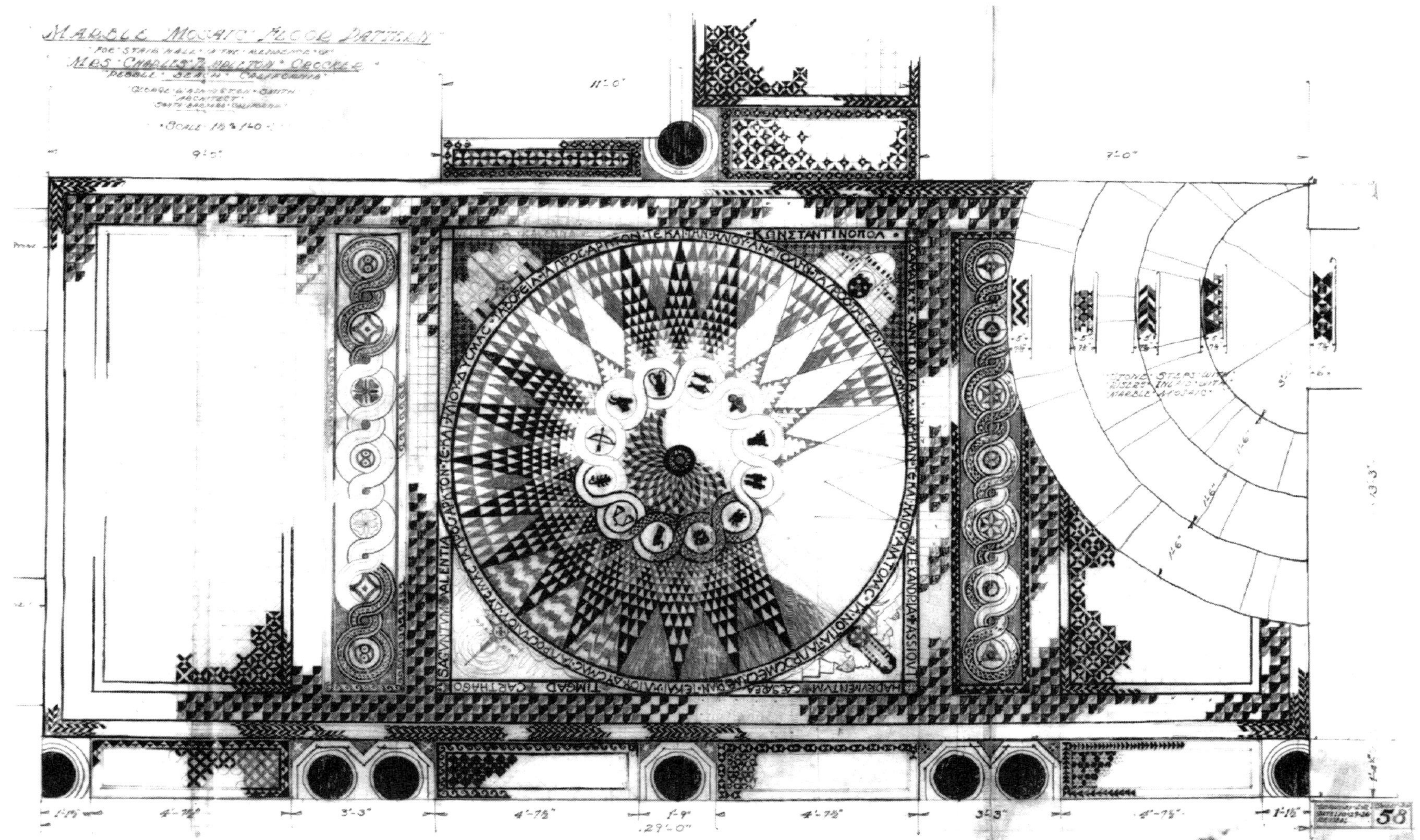
MARBLE MOSAIC FLOOR PATTERN
FOR STAIR HALL IN THE RESIDENCE OF
MRS. CHARLES TEMPLETON CROCKER
PEBBLE BEACH CALIFORNIA
GEORGE WASHINGTON SMITH
ARCHITECT
SANTA BARBARA CALIFORNIA
SCALE 1½"=1'-0"
STONE STEPS WITH RISERS INLAID WITH MARBLE MOSAIC
KΩNSTANTINOΠOΛ
58

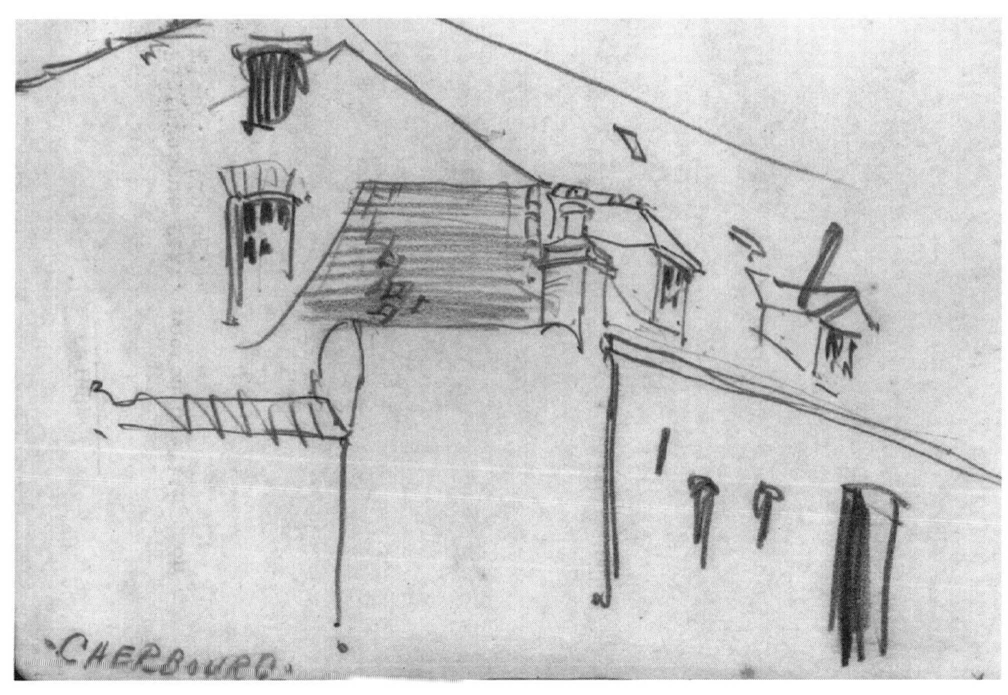
·CHERBOURG·

(Fig.22, opposite) Ink drawing for "A Small House in Brick" for the California Common Brick Manufacturers Competition, Fourth Prize, 1924

.*(Fig.21, opposite)* Conte crayon and pencil sketch of house in Cherbourg, France, 1928

(Fig. 23) Riggs house "Clavelitos," Montecito, 1926. (Photo: Fred R. Dapprich)

(Fig. 24 and 25) Riggs house: Clavelitos," Montecito, 1926. (Photo: Fred R. Dapprich)

(Fig. 27) Library addition, Steedman house, Montecito, 1929-33. (Photo: Marvin Rand)

(Fig. 28) J. Wesley Gallagher house, Montecito, 1930-31. (Photo: Fred R. Dapprich)

(Fig. 29, 30) J. Wesley Gallagher house, Montecito, 1930-31. (Photo: Fred R. Dapprich)

(Fig. 31) J. Wesley Gallagher house, Montecito, 1930-31. (Photo: Marvin Rand)

(Fig. 32) Pencil and conte crayon drawings for a Proj.: Mrs. Ellis Fischel house, Montecito, 1931.
(Fig. 33) Guest House.

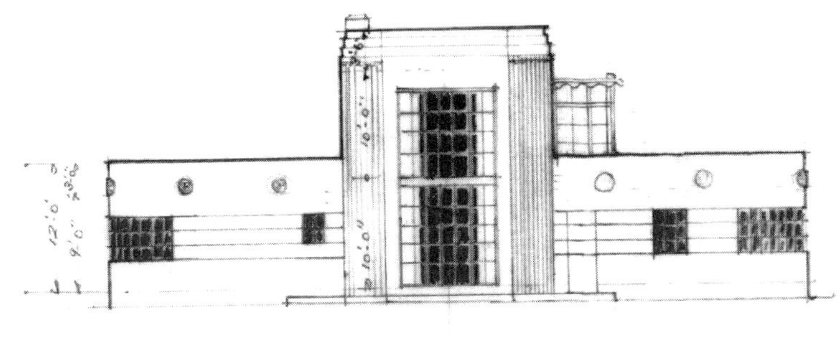

NORTH · ELEVATION

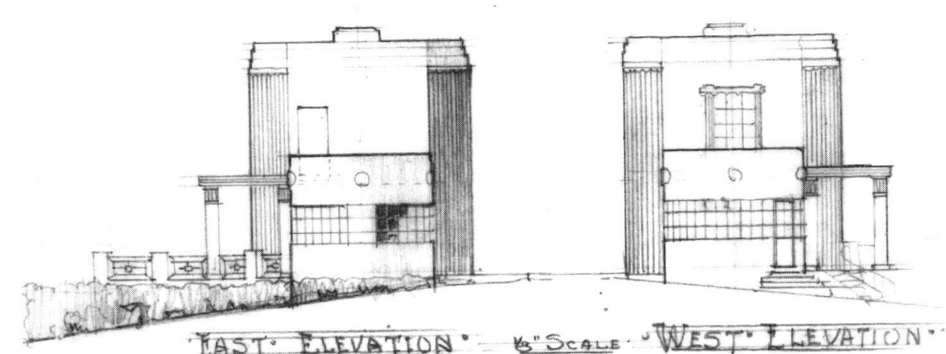

EAST · ELEVATION · ⅛" SCALE · WEST · ELEVATION

SOUTH · ELEVATION

· GUEST · HOUSE · FOR ·
· MRS · ELLIS · FISCHEL ·
· SANTA · BARBARA ·
· LUTAH · MARIA · RIGGS ·
· ARCHITECT ·
2 · DEC - 11 - 1931 ·
(= REVISION · OF · #1) ·

(Fig. 34, 35 and 36) Pencil and conte crayon drawing for Mrs. Daniel Murphy garden, Los Angeles, 1932-33 for A. E. Hanson.

(*Fig. 37*) Pencil drawings for a Proj.: House for House Beautiful magazine, 1932.

(*Fig. 38 and 39*) Allen Breed Walker house, Montecito, 1934-35. (Photo: Fred A. Dapprich)

NO

(Fig. 40 and 41) Allen Breed Walker house, Montecito, 1934-35. (Photo: Marvin Rand)

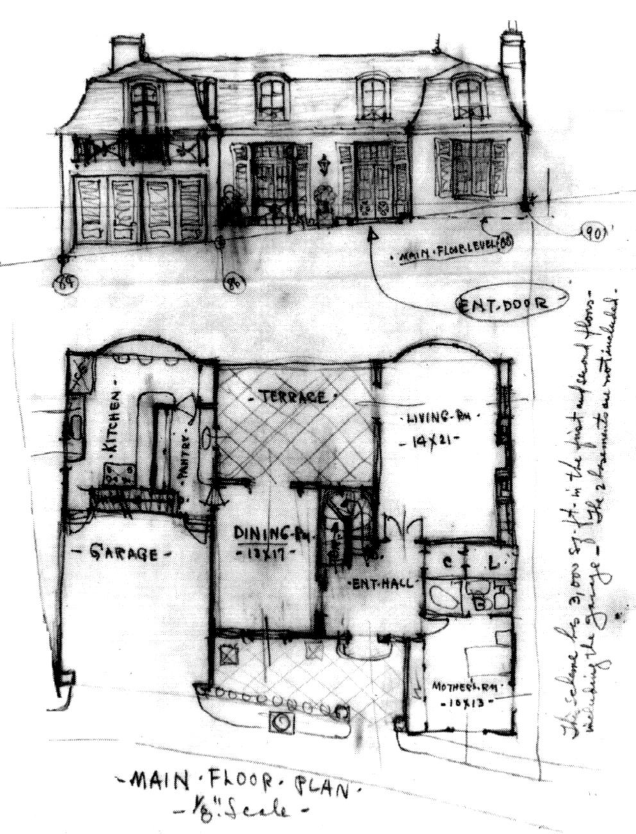

(Fig. 42) Pencil drawing for the Edgar Davy house, Los Angeles, 1935.

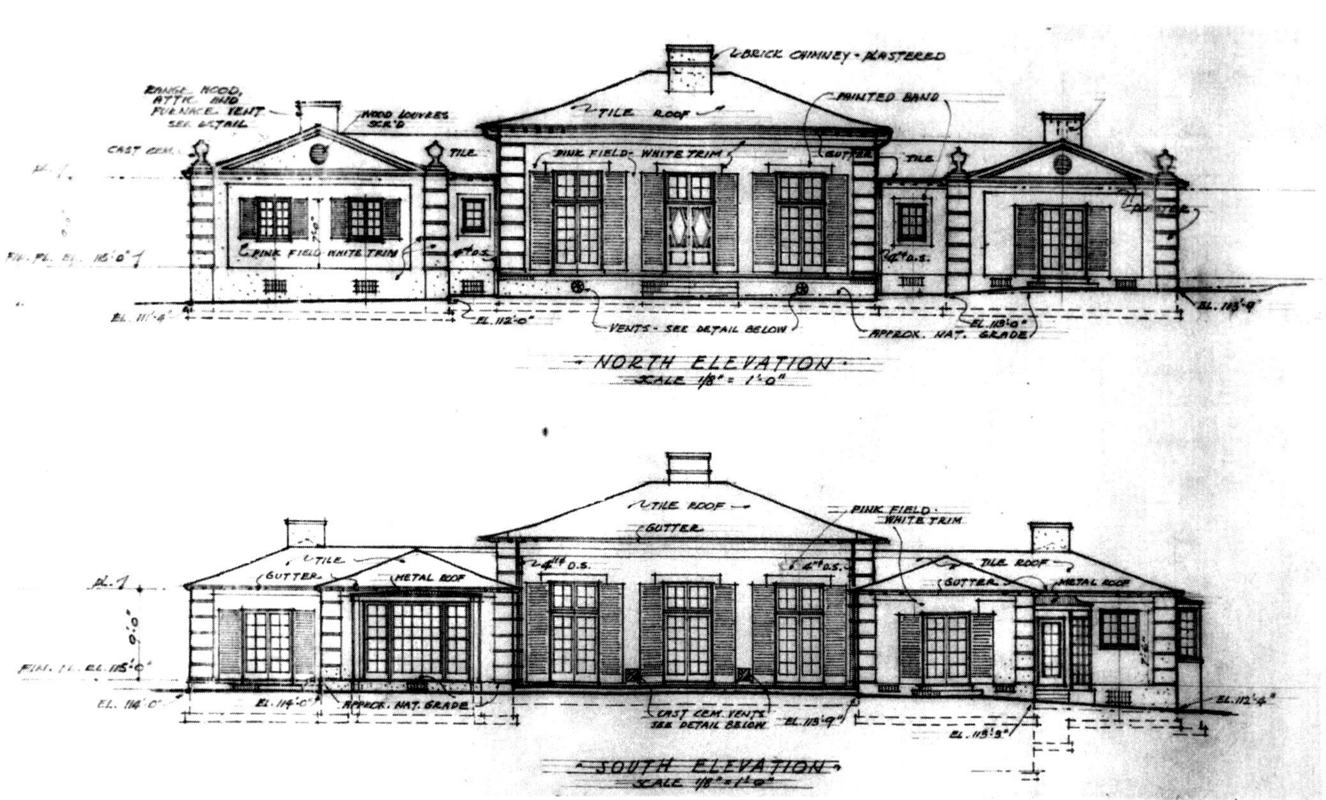

(Fig. 43) Working drawings for the Leon Graves house, Sherman Oaks, 1935-36.

(Fig. 44 and 45) Leon Graves house, Sherman Oaks, 1935-46. (Photo: Marvin Rand)

(Fig. 46 and 47) Pencil sketches of early design for the Baron Maximilian von Romberg house, Montecito, 1937.

(Fig. 48 and 49, opposite) Pencil perspective drawings of early study for the Baron Maximilian von Romberg house, Montecito, 1937.

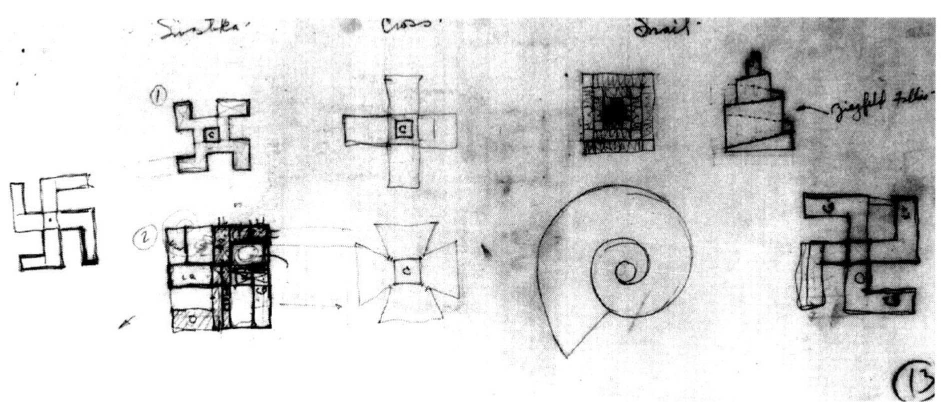

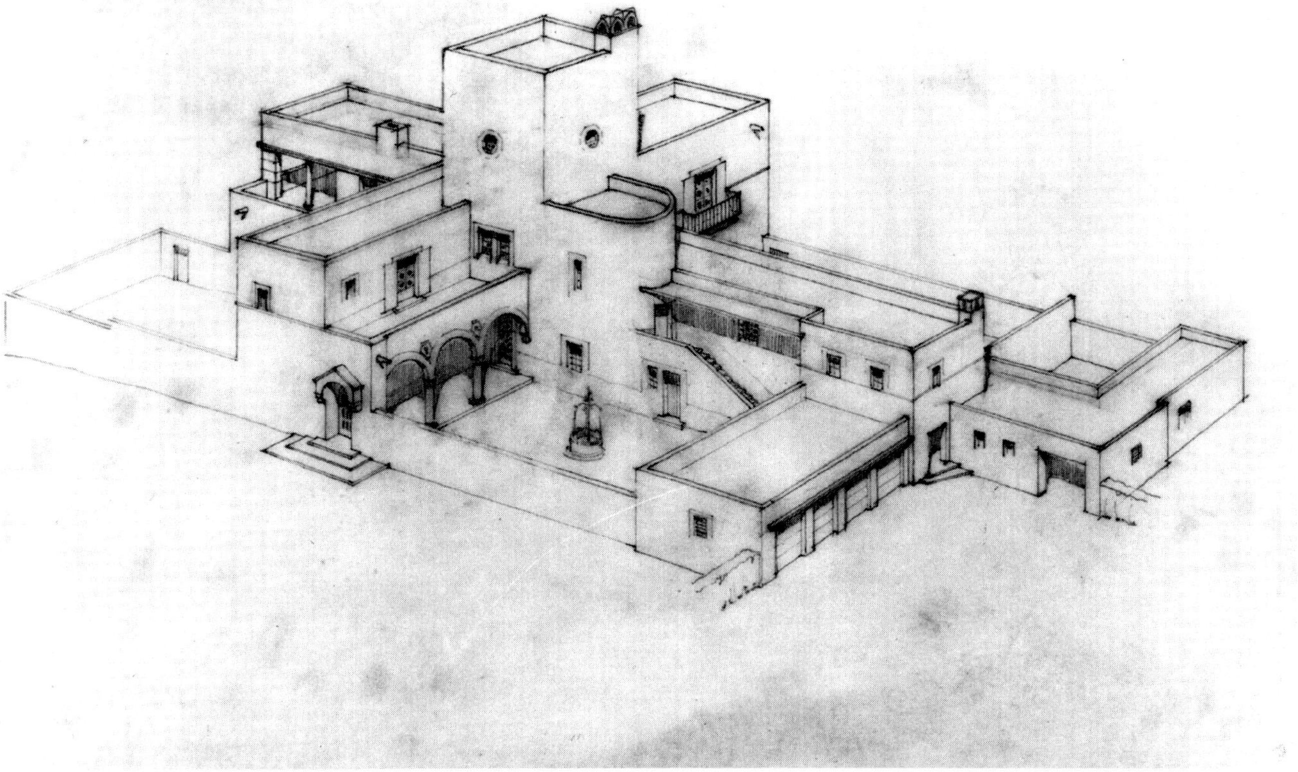

NORTH ELEVATION

(Fig. 51, 52 and 53) Baron Maximilian von Romberg house, Montecito, 1937-38. (Photo: Fred R. Dapprich)

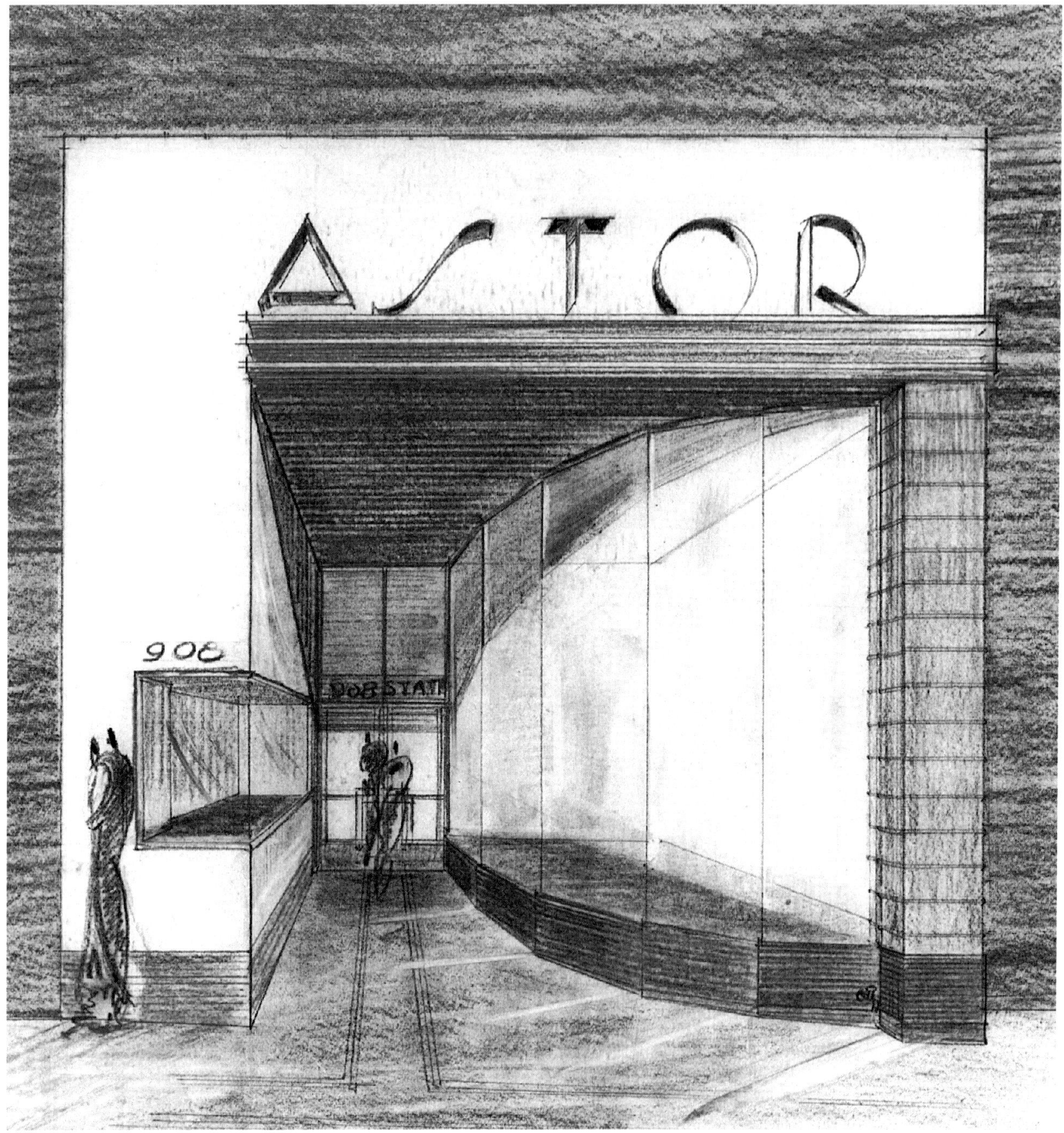

(Fig. 54) Watercolor drawing for Proj.: store front for "Astor," Santa Barbara, 1936-37.

(Fig. 55, left) A. E. Hanson house, Beverly Hills, 1939, 1941. (Photo: Marvin Rand)

(Fig. 56, bottom, left) Leonore Brooks house, Rolling Hills, 1939. (Photo: Marvin Rand)

(Fig. 57) Leonore Brooks barn, Rolling Hills, 1939. (Photo: Marvin Rand)

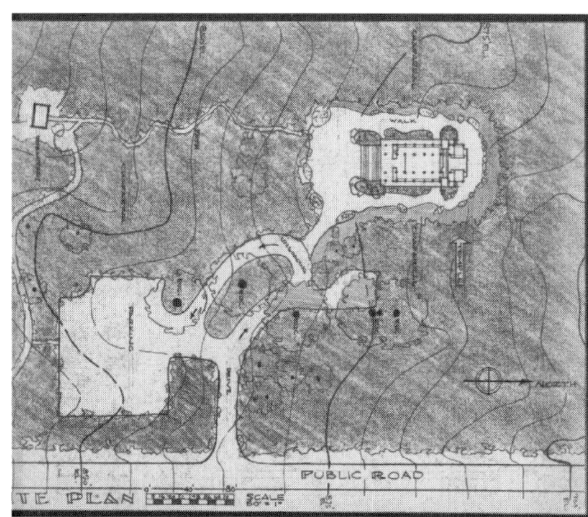

(Fig. 58) Walter P. Limacher house, "Flying Triangle," Rolling Hill, 1940. (Photot: Marvin Rand

(Fig. 60) Remodeling of house for Allen Breed Walker, Hollywood, 1941.

(Fig. 59) Remodeling of house for Allen Breed Walker, Hollywood, 1941.

(Fig. 61) Library and Herbarium for the Santa Barbara Botanic Garden, Santa Barbara, 1942. (Photo: Marvin Rand)

(Fig. 63 and 64) Film Stage Set for MGM Studios, "Picture of Dorian Gray." 1943. (Photo: courtesy of the Academy of Motion Picture Arts and Science, Beverly Hills.)

(Fig. 62, below) Pencil drawing for the Film Stage Set for MGM Studios, "Picture of Dorian Gray," 1943.

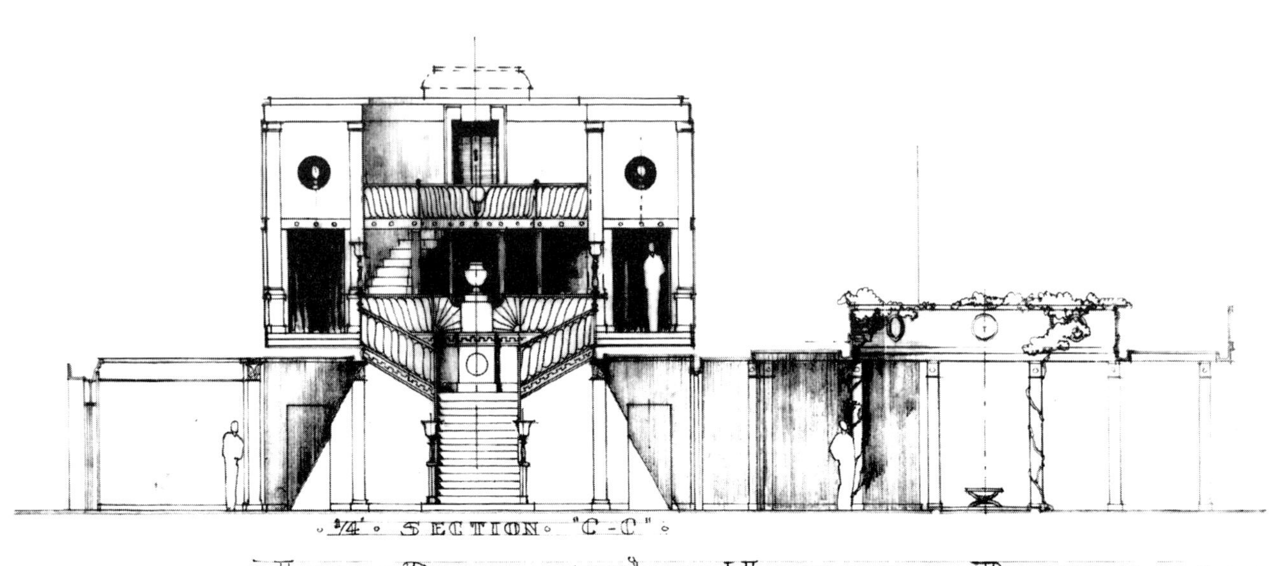

QUO VADIS
PLAUTIUS'

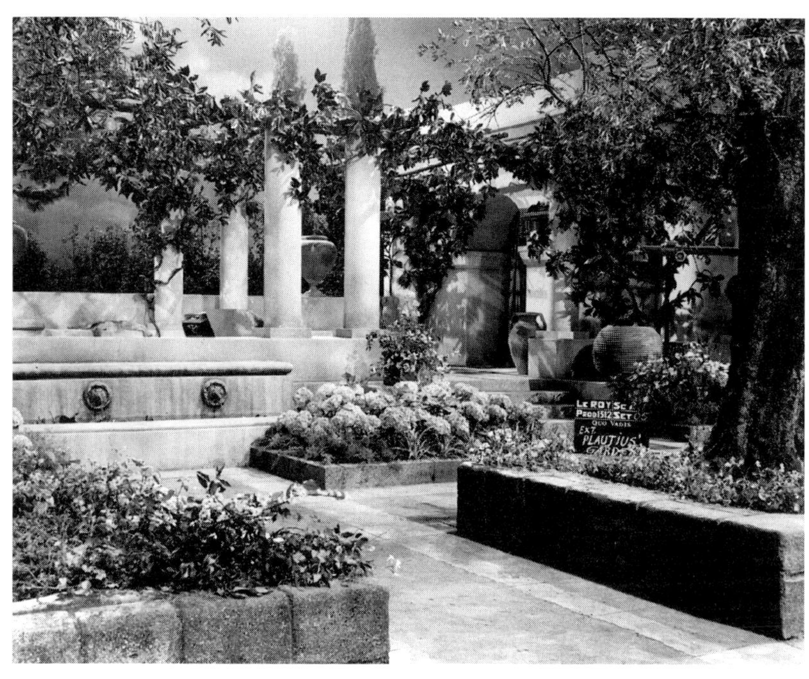

(Fig. 65) Film Stage Set for MGM Studios, "Quo Vadis," 1943. (Photo: courtesy of the Academy of Motion Picture Arts and Science, Beverly Hills.)

(Fig. 66) Pencil drawing for the Film Stage Set for MGM Studios, "The White Cliffs of Dover, 1943.

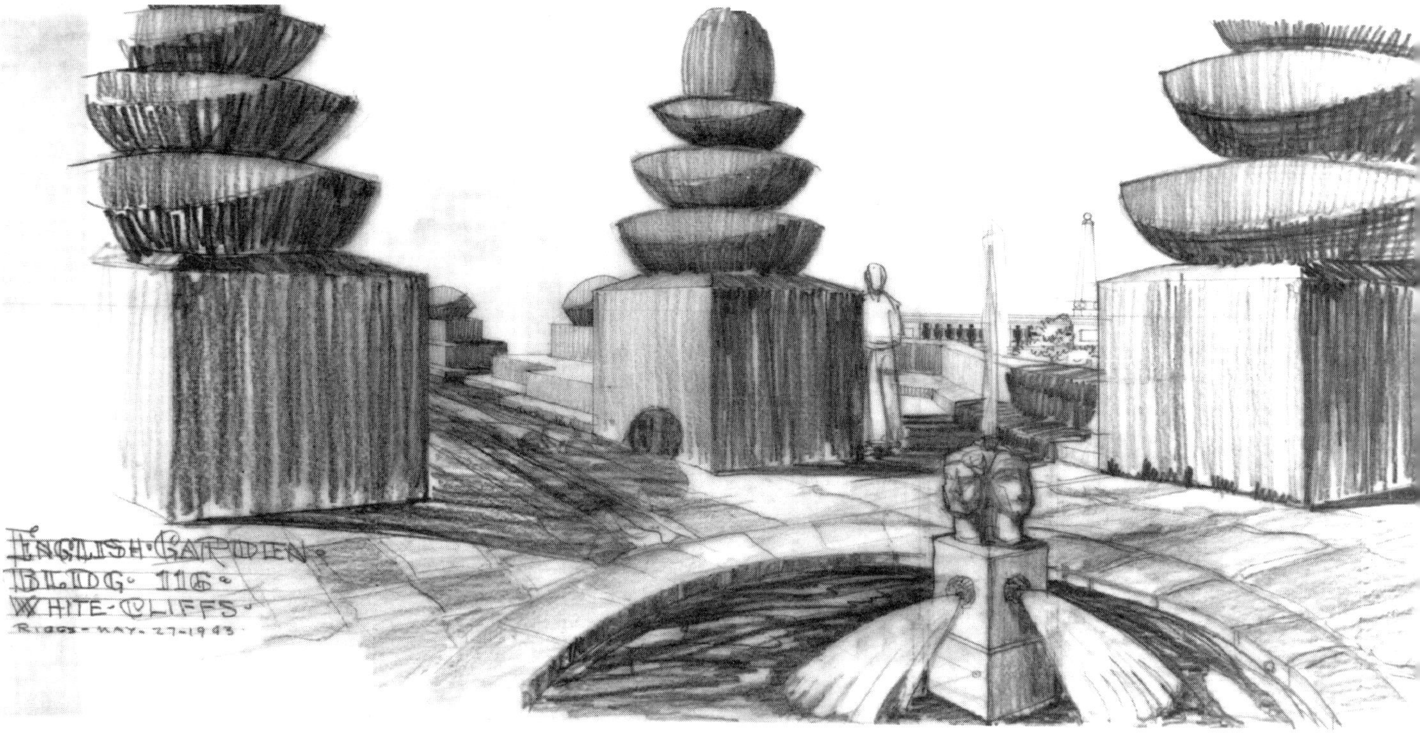
ENGLISH·GARDEN·
BLDG· 116·
WHITE·CLIFFS·
RIGGS - MAY - 27-1943

(Fig. 70) Pencil drawing for Proj.: Donald Kellogg beach house, Sandyland, Carpinteria, 1946.

(Fig. 68) Lutah Maria Riggs at the C. Pardee Erdman house, Montecito, 1966.

(Fig 67) Film Stage Set for MGM Studios "The White Cliffs of Dover," 1943. (Photo: courtesy of the Academy of Motion Picture Arts and Science, Beverly Hills.)

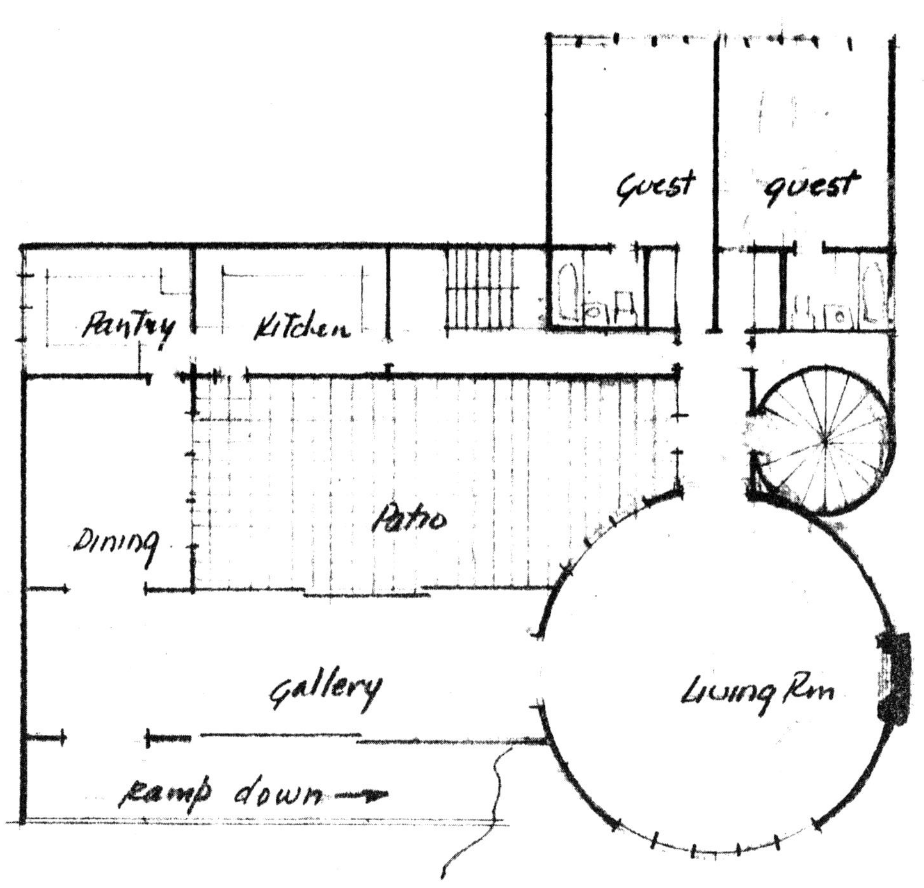
Guest
guest
Pantry
Kitchen
Patio
Dining
Gallery
Living Rm
Ramp down

(Fig. 71) Colored pencil drawing "Scheme A" for the Burton G. Tremaine, Jr. house, Serena Beach, 1947.

(Fig. 71A) Plot plan and floor plan of Tremaine house, Serena Beach, 1947.

(Fig. 72) Photo of model prepared by Oscar Neimeyer for the Burton G. Tremaine, Jr. house, Serena Beach, 1947, with Oscar Niemeyer; landscape design by Roberto Burle Marx. (Photo: Trayton Studios)

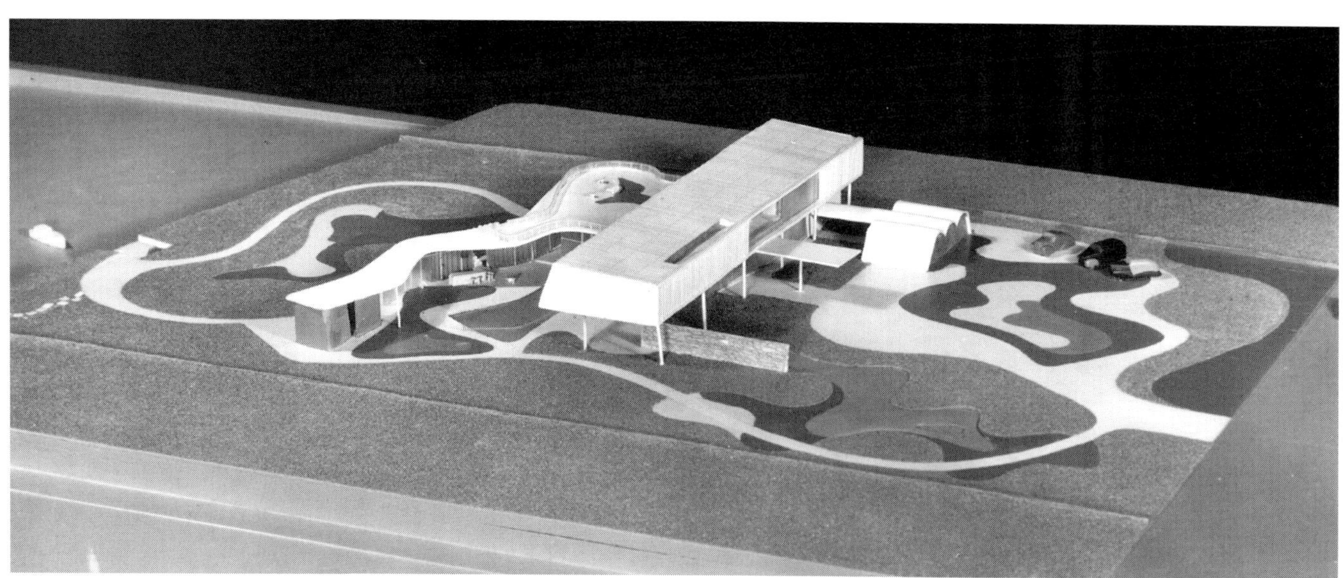

(Fig. 73) Model of the Burton G. Tremaine, Jr. ranch house, Winslow, Arizona

(Fig. 74) Detail of model of the Burton G. Tremaine, Jr. ranch house, Winslow, Arizona, 1947. (Photo: Joel Conway Studios)

(*Fig. 75)* Doyle W. Cotton house, Montecito, 1947-48; 1952; 1953. (Photo: Alice Erving)

(*Fig. 76)* Herman Baer house, Lompoc, 1947-49; 1953.

(Fig. 77) Beach Cooke house, Montecito, 1948.

(Fig. 78) Remodeling of house for Clinton Hollister, Santa Barbara, 1948, 1949-50, 1953. (Photo: Maynard L. Parker)

(Fig. 79) Robert E. Gross beach house, Sandyland Cove, Carpinteria, 1949, 1952-54, 1962-64. (Photo: Fred R. Dapprich)

(Fig. 80) Alice Erving house, Montecito, landscape by Thomas D. Church, 1949-51. (Photo: Marvin Rand)

(Fig. 81 and 82, oppostie) Alice Erving house, Montecito, 1949-51, landscape design by Thomas D. Church. (Photo: Alice Erving)

(Fig. 83) John B. Hamilton house, Montecito, 1951. (Photo: Marvin Rand)

(*Fig. 85)* Pencil on carbon reproduction for the site plan of the Vedanta Temple, Montecito, 1968.

(Fig. 84) Vedanta Temple, Montecito, 1954-56. (Photo: Marvin Rand)

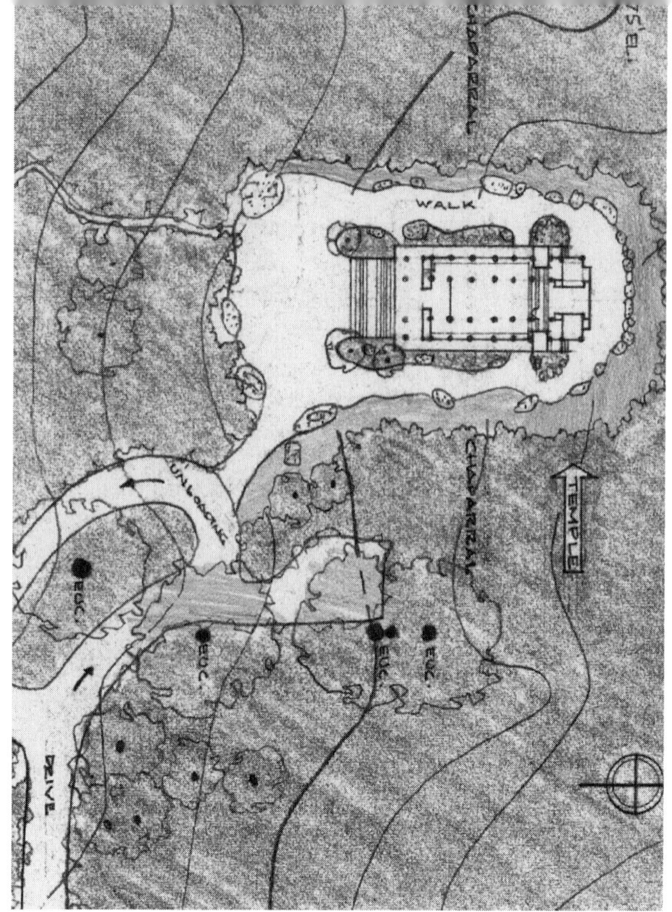

(Fig. 86 and 87) Vedanta Temple, Montecito, 1954-56. (Photo: Marvin Rand)

(Fig. 88, left) Vedanta Pavilion, Montecito, 1960, 1964-65. (Photo: Marvin Rand)

(Fig. 91) Garden for Daniel J. Donohue house "Villa San Giuseppe," Los Angeles, 1956-67. (Photo: Marvin Rand)

(Fig. 92) Garden for Daniel J. Donohue house "Villa San Giuseppe," Los Angeles, 1956-67. (Photo: Marvin Rand)

(Fig. 89) E. Leslie Kiler house, Santa Barbara, 1955. (Photo: Douglas M. Simmonds)

(Fig. 90) Remodeling of house for A. C. Pedotti, Santa Barbara, 1956. (Photo: Marvin Rand)

(Fig. 94, 95 and 96) C. Pardee Erdman house, Montecito, 1957-59. (Photo: Tomlinson Studio)

(Fig. 98, opposite) Wright S. Ludington house "Hesperides," Montecito, 1957-59. (Photo: Marvin Rand)

(Fig. 99) Wright S. Ludington house "Hesperides," Montecito, 1957-59. (Photo: Marvin Rand)

(Fig. 97) Wright S. Ludington house "Hesperides," Montecito, 1957-59. (Photo: Marvin Rand)

(Fig. 100) Peter Berkey III house, Carpinteria, 1961. (Photo: Richard Fish)

(Fig. 101) Alexander H. Teiers beach house, Sandyland Cove, Carpinteria, 1961-62.

(Fig. 102) Suski Building, Santa Barbara, 1964-65 (with Victor Gruen Assoc.) (Photo: Ray Borges)

(Fig. 103, opposite) Wright S. Ludington house "October Hill," 1973. (Landscape design by Elizabeth de Forest.) (Photo: Marvin Rand)

(Fig. 105, right) Wright S. Ludington house "October Hill," 1973. (Photo: Marvin Rand)

(Fig. 104, below) Wright S. Ludington house "October Hill," 1973. (Landscape design by Elizabeth de Forest.) (Photo: Marvin Rand)

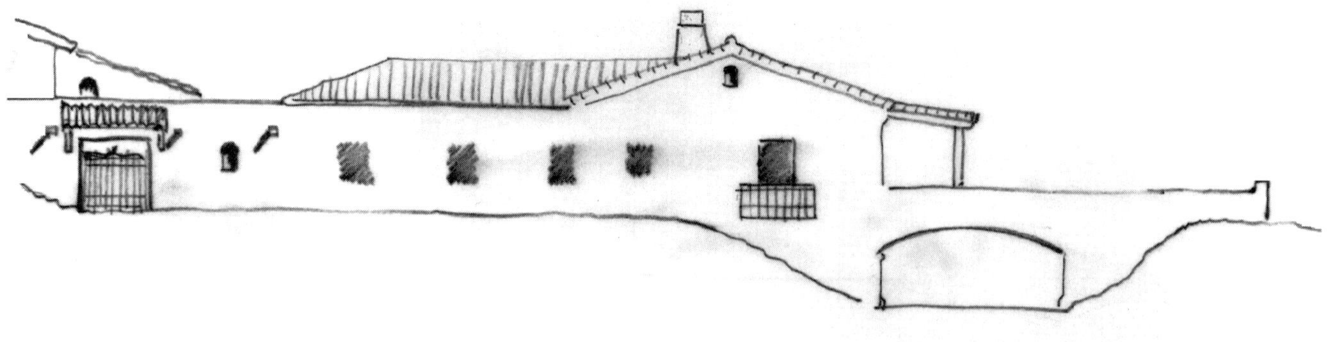

(Fig. 106) Pencil drawing for the Proj.: Eldon Haskell house, Santa Barbara County, 1977.

(Fig. 107) Jack C. Antrim house, Goleta, 1978-80. (Photo: Marvin Rand)

(Fig. 108) Conte crayon drawing of Lobero Theatre interior, 1923.

BARRYMORE
MR

Notes to Chapter One

1. "Baron Von Romberg Builds at Montecito." *Los Angeles Times* (May 23, 1937): Pt. V, p. 6.

2. Among Riggs's papers is a copy of an issue of *Bible Review: Advanced Esoteric Thought* 3:8 (May 1903). This magazine was published by the Esoteric Fraternity of Applegate, California.

3. Theo. Dickscheidt was listed in the 1918–1919 Santa Barbara City Directory as a Gardener, living at 407 N. Nopal Street.

4. *The Booster* 8: 2 (April 28, 1914): 5.

5. Notes in the collection of the Architectural Drawing Collection, University Art Museum, University California Santa Barbara.

6. Lutah Maria Riggs, "College Education," Compo. VII, March 1914 (LMR collection, ADC).

7. "Has College Really Helped Girls," *Ladies Home Journal* 29 (February 1912): 9; "Working One's Way Through College," *Review of Reviews* 46 (September 1912): 344–349.

8. Riggs used desk calendars, not only to indicate appointments, but, at times, almost as a diaries, from her days in high school in Ohio, on through the 1970s. While a number of these date calendars have survived, many have apparently been lost. The existing date calendars are extremely important in reconstructing many events of her life.

9. "Winner of News Prize is Doing Well at School," *Santa Barbara Daily News* (May 20, 1918): sec 2,7.

10. Sally Woodbridge, *Campus Historic Resources Survey* (Berkeley: University of California, 1978); Loren W. Partidge, *John Galen Howard and the Berkeley Campus: Beaux-Arts Architecture in the "Athens of the West"* (Berkeley: Berkeley Architectural Heritage Association, 1978); Sally Woodbridge (Editor), *Bay Area Houses* (Salt Lake City: Peregrine Smith Books, 1988): 76–80.

11. Surprisingly, there was no mention of William W. Wurster in Riggs's calendars for these years at Berkeley. Later in her life she mentioned Wurster quite often, indicating that on occasion he took her home from the Ark and so on.

12. Joan Draper, "The Ecole Des Beaux-Arts and the Architectural Profession in the United States: The Case of John Galen Howard," in Spiro Kostoff (Editor), *The Architect: Chapters on the History of the Profession* (New York: Oxford Univ. Press, 1977): 209–237.

13. John Galen Howard, "The Paris Training," *Architectural Review* (Boston) 5 (1898): 4–7; "The Spirit of Design at the Ecole des Beaux-Arts," *Architectural Review* 5 (1898): 25–27.

14. *The International Competition for the Phoebe Hearst Architectural Plan for the University of California* (San Francisco: Trustees of the Phoebe A. Hearst Architectural Plan for the Univertsity of California, 1899); Loren W. Partridge, *Op. cit.*: 4.

15. For a discussion of San Francisco's Bay Tradition see: Sally Woodbridge (editor), *Bay Area Houses* (Salt Lake City: Peregrine Smith, 1988).

16. William Charles Hays, *Order, Taste and Grace in Architecture* (Berkeley: Bancroft Library, Unpublished Manuscript of the Regional History Office, 1969).

17. Richard Chafee, "The Teaching of Architecture at the Ecole des Beaux-Arts," in Arthur Drexler (Editor), *The Architecture of the Ecole des Beaux-Arts* (Cambridge: MIT Press, 1977): 61–109; Russell Lynes, "A Grand School of Academic Design is Reexamined," *Smithsonian Magazine* 6 (November 1975): 79–86.

18. John Galen Howard, "The Spirit of Design at the Ecole des Beaux-Arts," *Architectural Review* (Boston) 5 (1898): 27.

19. Riggs's drafting on other drawings are mentioned in her calendars: "Worked on the Lee's plans," in May and June, 1920, and in July of the same year: "Worked on Prof. Langille's plans."

20. In her article, "A Walk With Lutah Maria Riggs," Esther McCoy quotes Riggs that after she returned from Susanville she worked for the architect, Theodore Spencer (*L.A. Architect* 5 [July 1979]: 3). Strangely, there is no mention of Spencer in Riggs' calendars from December 5 when she returned to Berkeley, until early August when she returned to Santa Barbara. It should be noted though, that there are only a few entries in her calendars from mid June through the end of July. Riggs mentioned that she drafted for Spencer when she was at Berkeley to this author as well, so she must have worked for him.

21. Taped interview of LMR, September 31, 1980, by Katherine McMahon (Tape #1).

22. William Lawrence Bottomsley, "The American Country House," *Architectural Record* 8 (October 1920): 258–272.

23. For a discussion of George Washington Smith see: Irving K. Morrow, "A Dialogue Which Touches on Mr. Smith's Architecture," *Architect and Engineer* 78 (July 1924): 53–97; John Taylor Boyd, Jr., "Houses Showing a Distinguished Simplicity," *Arts and Decoration* 33 (October 1930): 57–60, 112; David Gebhard, *George Washington Smith, 1876–1930, The Spanish Colonial Revival in Southern California* (Santa Barbara: University Art Museum, University of California, 1964); David Gebhard, "George Washington Smith," in Herb Andree and Noel Young (Editors), *Santa Barbara Architecture* (Santa Barbara: Capra Press, 1980): 88–111.

Notes to Chapter Two

1. Riggs's later memories of how Smith finally engaged her to work in his office and her brief period of teaching vary from her calendar entries. In later life Riggs often told the tale of the Smith's driving their big Lincoln up to the School (where she was ouside clapping chalkboard erasers), and he asked her to come back and work for him. No mention of this somewhat dramatic affair is contained in her Datebook for 1921. Also, see Verne Linderman, "Lutah Riggs, Santa Barbara's Only Licensed Woman Architect, Helped Create the Golden Era—the Era of Spanish Revival," *Santa Barbara News Press* (September 9, 1951): Sec A,3.

2. Riggs discussed her method of working with Smith in a taped interview dated May 23rd, 1982. This tape is in the ADC, U.C. Santa Barbara.

3. Lutah Maria Riggs, Datebooks, entry for December 19, 1922.

4. The jury for the competition was composed of three well-established Southern California architects: Sumner Spaulding, Pierpont Davis and Elmer Grey. The winning design was by Harrison Clarke; the second prize went to A. McD. McSweeney, and the third prize was awarded to W. F. Mullay. See Philip J. Meany, "Winners of the Small Brick House Competition," *Pacific Coast Architect* 25 (January 1924): 6–17; "Winning Designs in Brick Home Competition," *Architect and Engineer* 77 (January 1924): 73–80.

5. During the 1920s there were numerous articles and books published on the rural architecture of northern France. Two of these books which were in the library of George Washington Smith at the time that Riggs designed her entry for the Common Brick Competition were: Ralph Adams Cram, *Farm Houses, Manor Houses, Minor Chateaux, Small Churches in Normandy and Brittany* (New York: The Architectural Book Publishing Co., 1917) and Lewis Coffin, Jr., Henry M. Pelhemus, and Addison F. Worthington, *Small French Buildings* (New York: Scribners, 1921).

6. David Gebhard, "1915–1930—Traditionalism and Design: Old Models from the New," in Lisa Phillips (Editor), *High Style: Twentieth-Century American Design* (New York: Whitney Museum of Art, 1985): 48–81.

7. David Gebhard and Deborah Nevins, *200 Years of American Architectural Drawing* (New York: Whitney Library of Design, 1977): 228–229. Deborah Nevins and Robert A. M. Stern, *The Architects Eye: American Architectural Drawings from 1799–1979* (New York: Pantheon Books, 1979): 120–121.

8. Anne Stow-Fithian, "The Home of Miss Riggs, Montecito, California," *Home and Field* 40 (September 1930): 22; " 'Clavelitos,' The Home of Lutah Maria Riggs, Architect, in Santa Barbara," *California Arts and Architecture* 40 (July 1931): 28–29; "Kitchen in House at Santa Barbara, California, *American Architect* 147 (September 1935): 45–70.

9. Others who worked briefly in the mid 1920s in the GWS office were Carl Dumbolton, and Rolf Eskil.

10. Andrew N. Prentice, *Renaissance Architecture and Ornament in Spain* (New York: Paul Wenzel, n.d.): pl.

11. The design for the columns and their capitals came from the loggia of the patio of the Casa de Miranda in Burgos.

12. Riggs's involvement with the these two houses came after the design of each of them had already been established. She provided a number of drawings for the details of them.

Notes to Chapter Three

1. The partnership was announced in the *Architectural Forum* 52 (June 1930): 228. No notice in the architectural journals has been encountered indicating the end of the partnership.

2. Notes from an interview of author with Riggs, Jan. 12, 1979.

3. Steedman had discussed with Smith the idea of adding a small library room to the house, but there is no evidence that any drawings were made at that time (late 1929).

4. A. E. Hanson, *An Arcadian Landscape: The California Gardens of A. E. Hanson, 1920–1932* (Los Angeles: Hennessy and Ingalls, 1985): xiii.

5. Lutah Maria Riggs, Calendar entry for Wednesday, March 2, 1932.

6. Lutah Maria Riggs, Calendar for Friday, May 6, 1932.

7. Lutah Maria Riggs, Calendar entry for May 31, 1932.

8. Smith added a "French" room to the Edith Cunningham House, Monetcito (1926) and a French room and Boudoir to his remodeling of the George T. Cameron House in Burlingame (1928).

9. An announcement of the award of the contract for the von Romberg House was contained in the May 7th, 1937 issue of the *Southwest Builder and Contractor*, p. 60. The contractor for the project was O. J. Kenyon of Santa Barbara.

10. "Von Romberg is Killed in Plane Crash," *Santa Barbara News-Press* Sec. A, 1–2. "Air Crash Fatal to Baron Romberg," *The New York Times* (June 5, 1928): Pt. 1, p. 2).

Von Romberg was married in 1928 to Emily Hall in New York City. See: "Baron Von Romberg Weds Emily Hall," *The New York Times* (April 15, 1928): Pt. 2, p. 6.

11. In discussing the Von Romberg House in the late 1960's Lutah said that both Emily and Maximillian Von Romberg were highly involved with the design of the house. A list of the requirements for the house was drawn up by Emily which included such features as two offices (one for him and one for her), a future elevator, and a "secret stair from the Baron's office" to the upper floor.

12. Among the preliminary sketches for the von Romberg house are sets of drawings, numbered from 4 through 16. A number of these grouped drawings contain several different schemes. Lutah indicated when discussing these preliminary drawings in the late 1960s that this sequence from 4 through 16 indicates the chronology of the different approaches to the design. She could not recall why there were no sketches numbered 1 through 3, 7 and 14.

13. A. E. Hanson was brought in as a consultant on the von Romberg garden in late 1939. See: LMR, Datebook, September 19, 1939. "This coming week I am working free [for A.E. Hanson]—in return for Mr. Hanson's criticism on von Romberg—Spreckles garden and his trip to Santa Barbara to look at it."

14. The final Kent house in Montecito (1937) eliminated any direct references to the Streamline Moderne, leaving its image as that of the Hollywood Regency. Lutah worked on the design of this house with the Los Angeles firm of Plummer, Wurdeman and Becket. It was this latter firm who produced the working drawings.

15. "Mediterranean Sources Varied," *Santa Barbara News-Press* (March 3, 1940): Pt. 3, 17; "Beautiful Gillespie Estate Fine Example of Mediterranean Type," *Santa Barbara News-Press* (March 17, 1940): Pt. 3, 18.

16. A. E. Hanson, *Rolling Hills: The Early Years* (Rolling Hills: City of Rolling Hills, 1978).

17. "Hedda Hopper's Hollywood," *Los Angeles Times* (June 14, 1939): Pt. 1, p. 12; "Local Architect Aids Greta Garbo Build," *Santa Barbara News-Press* (June 14, 1939): Pt. 1, p. 8. In her calendar for Monday, December 24, 1933, she notes that she drove down to La Quinta east of Palm Springs. On the following day that "Garbo telephones that she is coming down with George Bent, incognito . . ."

18. A. E. Hanson, *Op.cit.* 1978: 78.

19. David Gebhard, "The American Colonial Revival in the 1930s," *Winterthur Portfolio* 22 (Summer/Autumn 1987): 109–148.

20. David Gebhard, "Introduction," in Sally Woodbridge (Editor), *Bay Area Houses* (Salt Lake City: Peregrine Smith, 1988): 3–23; Richard Peters, "William Wilson Wurster: An Architect of Homes," also in Woodbridge: 121–153.

21. David Gebhard and Harriette Von Breton, *Los Angeles in the Thirties: 1931–1941* (Los Angeles: Hennesey and Ingalls, 1989): 98–99.

22. LMR, *Datebook, 1940* entry for April 6, 1940.

23. L.M.R., Calendar, Friday, October 3, 1941.

24. Lutah Maria Riggs, letter to Genevieve Keighley, dated May 15th, 1941. Lutah Maria Riggs Collection, Architectural Drawing Collection, University Art Museum, Univ. California, Santa Barbara.

25. Lutah Maria Riggs, letter to Genevieve Keighley, dated May 15th, 1941.

26. LMR Datebook, 1942: entry for September 12, 1942.

27. LMR Datebook 1942; entry for September 14, 1942.

28. Another of her film sets for MGM was an "English Garden," for *White Cliffs of Dover*.

29. LMR Datebook for 1943, entry for December 17, 1943.

30. Regrettably, Lutah's records do not provide us with a list of all of the films for which she helped design stage sets. For a listing of the MGM films produced during those years, see: Douglas Eames, *The MGM Story* (New York: Crown Publishers, Inc., 1979); for the years 1943 through 1945: 184–205. Riggs mentions working also for Warner Brothers during the late war years. See: Ted Sennett, *Warner Brothers Presents* (New Rochelle, N.Y.: Arlington House, 1971); for the years, 1943 through 1945: 398–404.

31. LMR, Datbook for 1943, entry for March 23, 1943.

32. LMR, Datebook for 1943, entry for March 24, 1943.

Notes to Chapter Four

1. Walter Landor, "West Coast U.S.A.—Post War," *Architect's Yearbook:3* (London, 1949):130.

2. *Ibid.*: 130.

3. Elizabeth Mock (editor), *Built in USA: 1932–1944* (New York: Museum of Modern Art, 1944); Henry Russell Hitchcock and Arthur Drexler (Editors), *Built in USA: Post-war Architecture* (New York: Simon and Schuster, 1952).

4. Walter Landor, *Op.cit.*: 130.

5. Wayne Andrews, *Architecture, Ambition and Americans* (New York: Harper and Brothers, 1955): 252–256.

6. David Paul Bricker, *Built for Sale: Cliff May and the Low Cost California Ranch House.* (Santa Barbara, Unpublished M.A. Thesis, University of California, 1983).

7. Before he went on to Yale for his architectural studies Shaw had worked as a young draftsperson in Riggs's office in 1937. During his first summer break from Yale, he worked again for Riggs in 1938. He was initially introduced to Riggs through mutual friends that know his Pasadena parents. Arvin B. Shaw was credited as one of the designers of the United Nations Building in New York. See: "UN Rites Climax Shaw's Role in Structure's Plans," *Santa Barbara News-Press* (October 24, 1949): Sec. A, 3.

8. "How to be Carefree without Roughing It." *House and Garden* 119 (June 1961): 80–89. "Dune Dwelling," *The New York Times Magazine* Sec. 6 (June 26, 1960): 34–35.

9. Richard B. Nelson joined Riggs in November, 1948, and remained with her until June, 1964.

10. Walter Landor, *Op.cit.*: 130; Lewis Mumford, "The Skyline," *The New Yorker* 23 (October 11, 1947): 94–96.

11. A. Quincy Jones and Frederick E. Emmons, *Builders Homes for Better Living* (New York: Reinhold Publishing Corp., 1957); Whitney R. Smith and Wayne Williams, "Case Study House No. 12," *Arts and Architecture* 63 (December 1946}: 39, and "House, Pasadena, California," *Progressive Architecture* 28 (June 1947): 56. Cliff May (and the Editorial Staff of Sunset Magazine), *Sunset Ranch Houses* (Menlo Park: Land Publishing Co., 1946).

12. Richard C. Peters, "William Wilson Wurster: An Architect of Homes," and Sally Woodbridge, "From Large-Small House to Large-Large House," in Sally Woodbridge (Editor), *Bay Area Houses* (Salt Lake City: Peregrine Smith Books, 1988): 121–227.

13. "Designed with Simplicity and Taste to Melt into the Landscape," *Book of Homes* 14 (1958): 39–41.

14. "Designed into this Country House . . . Comfort in Its Looks and Living," *Sunset* 109 (July 1952): 52–53. The house was also featured in the *Santa Barbara News-Press* (March 12, 1950): Sec D,3, "New Montecito Residence of Mrs. Beach Cooke has Bright, Cheerful Design."

15. "Gross Beach House, Sandy Land Cove," *Sunset* 104 (May 1950): 36–37; "Simplicity and Livability Stressed in Beach Home of Mr. and Mrs. Robert Gross," *Santa Barbara News-Press* (May 21, 1950): Sec D,3.

16. "Gross Beach House, Sandy Land Cove," *Sunset* 104 (May 1950): 36–37. The Gross house was featured as the colored cover for this issue of the magazine.

17. Remarks of LMR to the author, during the summer of 1964.

18. Stamo Papadaki, *The Work of Oscar Niemeyer* (New York: Reinhold Publish Corp., 1950): 188. The house was presented in this book through sketches and photographs of a model. Its plan and elevations matches the drawings being produced by Riggs and Shaw.

19. "Santa Barbara, Project for a House," *Arts and Architecture* 66 (March 1949): 26–29.

20. "Glass Tent, A Santa Barbara House," *House and Home* 2 (September 1952): 114–119; Roberto Aloi, *Camini D'Oggi.* (Milan: Ulrico Hoepli, 1957): 156.

21. Letter of Alice Erving to LMR, dated December 2, 1944; 1–2. Riggs Collection, ADC, Univ. Art Museum, U.C. Santa Barbara.

22. *Ibid.*: 2.

23. By the time work had begun on the Erving project, Alice Erving and her mother (Mrs. J. Langdon Erving, had decided to build two separate houses. The small house for Mrs. Erving (also designed by Riggs), sited to the north of the Alice Erving house, was built in 1950.

24. "Glass Tent, A Santa Barbara House" *House and Home* 2 (September 1952): 113–114.

25. Conversation of Alice Erving with the author at her house in September, 1961.

26. Riggs worked with the landscape architect Thomas Church on several other projects, including the the Erdman House, Montecito, 1958.

27. "Opera Shed," *Progressive Architecture* 28 (March 1947): 53–58.

Notes to Chapter Five

1. "California's Competition for the Design of the Governor's Mansion," *Architectural Record* 131 (February 1962): 23; "California's Governor's Mansion," *Progressive Architecture* 43 (April 1962): 59.

2. David Gebhard, "The Governor's Mansion Competition," *Art Forum* 1 (1962): 34–35.

3. Comments of LMR concerning the 1949 Caribbean trip, made to the author in 1963.

4. Joseph Knowles first entered LMR's office in 1965. He left in December for the Vietnam War and returned in 1968.

5. The gardens of the Erdman House were designed by Thomas Church.

6. Esther McCoy, *Modern California Houses* (New York: Reinhold Pub. Corp., 1962): See especially the Triade development, La Jolla, 1959–60; 160–187.

7. "In Santa Barbara, an unusual remodel . . . With the quite charm of an old Spanish ranch house . . ." *Sunset* 119 (September 1957): 54–57.

8. *Ibid.*, 55. The editors of *House Beautiful* 101 (November 1959): 295, responded to the design in a similar fashion: "Imaginative planning turned an old Spanish-style bungalow and its detached garage into a contemporary house."

9. Craig designed the complex in 1922. When he died in that year, the project was take on by his wife Mary Osborne Craig and by his associate, Carlton M. Winslow. The shopping area centered on a small interior courtyard and an open patio-oriented restaurant. These spaces were connected to the public streets to the east, south and west via romantic narrow paseos. The Suski's as the new owner of the complex decided to provide a more open Paseo entrance from State Street and also to enhance the use of the property by building a five story office building to the north.

10. Conversation of the author with LMR in July, 1964.

11. In 1960 Riggs designed the lanterns for the Temple. Other buildings designed by her within the Vedanta Temple compound were a Gatehouse (1958–59, 1963; a Pavilion (1960, 1964–65); a Carport (1960); and the Eva Herrmann House (1968–70).

12. Edward S. Morse, *Japanese Houses and Their Surroundings* (Boston: Ticknor & Co., 1886); Ralph Adams Cram, *Impressions of Japanese Architecture* (Boston: Marshall Jones Co., 1905, 1930). The more recent literature in the Riggs's library included Osvald Siren, *Gardens of China* (New York: Ronald Press, 1949).

13. "The E. C. Anthony House, Los Angeles," *Architectural Digest* 8 (1931): 93–101; "The Earl C. Anthony House," *Country Life* 79 (May 1929): 71–72.

14. Kenneth H. Cardwell, *Bernard Maybeck: Artisan, Architect, Artist* (Salt Lake City: Peregrine Smith, 1977):219–229.

15. Mark Daniels "Another Anthony Occupies His Niche," *California Arts and Architecture* 39 (May 1931): 21–23,62–63.

16. *Ibid.*:62.

17. *Ibid.*: 62.

18. Edith Wharton, *Italian Villas and Their Gardens* with Pictures by Maxfield Parrish (New York: The Century Co., 1903 and 1904). A copy of the 1904 edition was in LMR's library.

19. These two houses, together with other late 1970s design were in fact joint projects designed by LMR and Joseph Knowles.

Notes to Chapter Six

1. Lutah Maria Riggs, "Geo. Washington Smith, A Tribute," *Architect and Engineer* 101 (April 1932): 89.

2. Comments of LMR to the author when he was working in her office in 1962 preparing an exhibition of George Washington Smith to be held in 1964 at the Art Galleries (now University Art Museum), University of California Santa Barbara.

3. These comments about the feminist view of her as a woman in architecture were mentioned by LMR to the author from time to time in the decade of the 1970s.

4. "The Woman Architect," *Architect and Engineer* 30 (October 1912): 103. Though the author of this article was open to women in the practice of architecture, there are the usual inuendos which makes one wonder how full was his commitment to the idea.

5. "A Thousand Women in Architecture," *Architectural Record* 103 (March 1948): 105–113), (June 1948): 108–115).

6. For Victorine Homsey (she practiced with her husband, Samuel): "Cambridge Yacht Club," *Architectural Forum* 69 (October 1938): 254–256; "Community Recreation Center, Seaford, Delaware," *Architectural Forum* 70 (July 1942): 29–30). Two examples of the published work of Verna Cook Shipway see: "Ernest Greenwood House at Scarsdale, New York," *House and Garden* 70 (Section II) September 1936): 137; "Formal Georgian House," *Pencil Points* 16 (February 1935): 75.

7. Harriet Rochlin, "A Distingished Generation of Women Architects in California," *Journal of the American Institute of Architects* 66 (August 1977): 38.

8. Verna Cook Salamonsky, "Woman Architect Gives Views," *Southwest Builder and Contractor* 88 (August 14, 1936):19.

9. Lutah Riggs, "George Washington Smith, A Tribute," *Architect and Engineer* 101 (April 1932): 89.

PROJECTS AND BUILDINGS
(A Selected List)

1924
Proj.: Common Brick Small House Competition, Fourth Prize.

1926
Riggs, Lutah Maria residence, "Clavelitos," Montecito

1930
Proj.: Andrews, William H. residence, Montecito

Douglas, Malcolm, Montecito (entrance gates)

Gallagher, J. Wesley residence, Montecito

Jackling, Daniel C. residence, Woodside (alterations)

Steedman, George F. residence (original residence by George Washington Smith), Montecito (library additions & alterations, 1930-33)

Proj.: House Design for *House Beautiful* (magazine)

Proj.: House Design for *Good Housekeeping* (magazine)

1931
Baldwin, Mrs. Lester guest cottage, Montecito

Davis, Mrs. Norris King residence, Montecito (alterations)

Fischel, Mrs. Ellis residence Santa Barbara

1932
Knight, Samuel residence, Montecito (alterations and additions, 1932-33)

1933

Edwards, F.B. residence, Santa Barbara (alterations)

Eicheim, Henry residence (original residence by George Washington Smith), Montecito (alterations, 1933-34, 1937)

1934
Courtney-Ravenscroft, Mrs. Jeffrey S. residence (original residence by George Washington Smith), Montecito (alterations & additions)

Myrick, Donald beach cottage, Sandyland Cove, Carpinteria (alterations & additions)

Walker, Allen Breed residence, Montecito (Butler's cottage & glass house, 1934-35)

1935
Proj.: Davey, Edgar residence, Los Angeles

Proj.: Gertzen, Samuel Stark residence, Los Angeles (1935-36)

Graves, Leon residence, Los Angeles (1935-36)

1936
Proj.: Astor Shop for the Burke building, Santa Barbara

Cooper, William residence, Montecito

Proj.: Smith, Mrs. George Washington (Mary) residence Tuscon, Arizona

1937
Biltmore Hotel, Montecito (bath house)

Proj.: Breckenridge, Mrs. John C. residence, Santa Barbara (1937-38)

Hall, Mrs. William H., Montecito (alterations)

Proj.: Jackson, Newton residence Los Altos (1937-38)

Parrot, Kent Kane residence, Montecito (with Plummer, Wurdeman & Becket) (1937-39)

Proj.: Stow, Mrs. Edgar weekend cottage Santa Ynez Mountains

Stow, Edgar ranch cottage, Patera Rancho, Goleta (1937-38)

Von Romberg, Baron Maximilian residence Montecito (1937-38; 1939-40)

Black, G. Palmer & Louise residence, Santa Barbara (additions, 1938, 1942)

Proj.: Santa Barbara Mutual Bldg. & Loan Assoc., Santa Barbara, (Model Small House)

Spalding, Mrs. G.L. residence, Santa Barbara (alterations)

Proj.: Woodyatt, Roland F. residence, Burnham Park, Evanston, Illinois (1938-40)

1939
Alexander, Taylor residence, Rolling Hills

Banta, F.N. residence, Rolling Hills

Brooks, Lenore residence, Rolling Hills

Proj.: Burke, Margaret Apartment Building, Palm Springs (not dated, c. 1939?)

Johnson, Carl M. residence, Rolling Hills (proj.?)

Gasoline Service Station Rolling Hills

Chadwick Seaside School, Palos Verdes (landscape design, alteration & additions, 1939-40)

Denni, Joseph A. residence, Rolling Hills

Dudley, Edward C. residence, Rolling Hills

Hanson, A.E. Co., Developers, "Williamsburg house," spec. residence, Rolling Hills (design by LMR, consultant; Victor E. Siebert-chief architect)

Hanson, A.E. Co., Developers, Spec Residence #1-B, Harbor Hills

Hanson, A.E. residence, Beverly Hills (alterations & additions, not dated, c. 1939?; garage addition 1941)

Hix, Clifton A. residence, Rolling Hills

Johnson, Carl M. residence, Rolling Hills

Johnson, Elwood residence, Rolling Hills

Knemeyer, C.V. residence, Rolling Hills

Pearson, O.W. residence, Rolling Hills

Rolling Hills Estates Administration Building, Rolling Hills (additions)

Serpell, George residence, Rolling Hills

Silveria, Joseph residence & stable, Rolling Hills (1939-40)

Proj.: Unidentified house for Williamsburg Lane, Rolling Hills

1940
Proj.: Church of Jesus Christ of Latter Day Saints San Pedro (alterations and additions)

Cohu, Lamotte residence, Rolling Hills Davis, Mrs. Charles W. residence,Santa Barbara

Graye, J.A. residence, Rolling Hills

Jefferson, John Percival, Montecito (alterations, card room & roof garden)

Limacher, Walter P. residence "Flying Triangle",Rolling Hills

Perkins, Mrs. Walter residence, Santa Barbara

Ramelli, Mattie residence, San Bernardino (1940-41)

Raub, Chester residence, Rolling Hills

Serns, Arthur residence, Santa Barbara additions & alterations

Westfield, houses #1 & #2, Rolling Hills

1941
Walker, Allen Breed residence, Hollywood (alterations & additions)

Proj.: Keighley, William Residence, Toluca Lake,North Hollywood

1942
Ravenscroft, Harry & Elsie ranch house, Goleta (alterations)

Santa Barbara Botanic Gardens, (library & herbarium)

Metro-Goldwyn-Mayer Studios, film sets 1942-45 *Picture of Dorian Gray, White Cliffs*

1945
Proj.: Barrett, Edna residence, Santa Barbara

Bissell, Arthur D. residence, Santa Barbara

Comparte, A .J. residence, Los Angeles (1945-46)

Proj.: Cottage Hospital, Santa Barbara (penthouse for east wing)

Proj.: Francis, J. Dwight residence, Montecito (alterations and additions)

Kairne, Mary B. residence, San Marino (alterations)

Proj.: Mitchell, Stanley residence, Montecito

Proj.: Parrot, Kent K. residence (house #1), Carmel (1945-46)

Parsons, Suzanne office, Santa Barbara (alterations)

Stow-Fithian, Anne, Santa Barbara (alterations and additions)

Hesse, Paul A., farm house, Rancho Topanga, Malibu (not dated; c. 1945?)

1946
Proj.: Ballard, Mrs. B. residence, Santa Barbara County

Proj.: Bogeaus, Benedict, Beverly Hills (addition, game room)

Briggs, Mrs. Walter residence, Santa Barbara (alterations)

Brooksbank, Percy A. residence, Folded Hills Ranch, Gaviota

Foster, Norman residence, Beverly Hills (alterations)

Green, John H., Montecito (alterations and additions, conversion of water tank tower into living quarters)

Harvey, Katherine residence, Montecito (alterations)

Humphries, Catherine residence, Carpinteria

Hutton-Miller, W.E. residence, "Puerto Limon," Montecito
Keeney, Mrs. Fred C. residence, Santa Barbara

Kellogg, Donald beach cottage, Montecito

Proj.: Kiam, Omar, Montecito (addition of pool house, swimming pool, and garden)

Lyttle, John residence, Ojai (1946-48)

McDuffie, Malcolm residence, Montecito (addition of a cottage)

Morton, Wirt residence, Montecito (addition of a guest house)

Nugent, Daniel beach cabana, Montecito

Parsons, Suzanne R. residence, Santa Barbara 1946-47)

1947
Armstrong, Horace W. residence, Santa Barbara (alterations & addition of a guest house, 1947, 1953)

Parrot, Kent Kane residences, Carmel (houses No. 2 & 3, 1947-48)

Baer, Herman residence, Lompoc (additions, dressing rooms for swimming pool, windbreak for pool, 1947-49, 1953)

Cotton, Doyle W. residence, Montecito (alterations, addition of guest house, shelter for north terrace, 1947-1953)

Forbstein, Leo residence, Beverly Hills (alterations)

Griffin, Francis residence, Bel Air (alterations)

Proj.: Hauser, Lewis A., apartments, Los Angeles

Holt, Mrs. William Leland residence, Santa Barbara

Johnson, Mrs. Elsie residence, Montecito (1947-48)

Lewis, Mrs. Carl (Betty) residence, Montecito (alterations)

Proj.: Montecito Shopping Center, (1947-48)

O'Melveny, Stuart residence, Sandyland Cove,Carpinteria (1947-50, 1952)

Peterson, Andrew residence #1, Buellton

Proj.: Prud'Homme, Rhonda shops, Montecito (1947-49)

Santa Barbara Museum of Art, Santa Barbara (alterations & additions , 1947, 1952-54)

Proj.: Serena Beach Club, Montecito

Proj.: Tevis, Lloyd residence, Carmel
Proj.: Tremaine, Burton G. Jr. residence, Serena Beach (Oscar Niemeyer architect, Lutah Maria Riggs, Associated)

Proj.: Tremaine, Burton G. Jr. ranch house, "Meteor-Crater Ranch, nr. Winslow, Arizona, 1946-47

Proj.: Weld, George residence, Santa Barbara (1947-48)

1948
Armstrong, Earl V. residence, Montecito (1948-49)

Cooke, Beach residence, Montecito

Hall, Purdon Smith residence, Montecito (alterations)

Hollister, Clinton residence, Santa Barbara (additions, 1948, 1949-50, 1953)

Hollister, Joseph J. residence, Gaviota

Kitchell, Howell W. residence, Montecito

Kolyn, Paul residence, Santa Barbara (1948-49; 1954, 1959)

Milholland, J.C., residence, Montecito (alterations)

Nelson, Lawrence M. residence, Santa Barbara (alterations)

Proj.: Struthers, James residence, Montecito

Wack, John T. DeBlois residence, Hope Ranch addition of stables, barns & cottages, 1948-49)

Proj.: Westwick, Judge & Mrs. residence, Santa Barbara

White, Harwood A., beach cottage, Sandyland Cove, Carpinteria (alterations)

1949
Cowlishaw, Ruth W. residence, Montecito (alterations)

Erving, Mrs. J. Langdon & Ms Alice, residences, Montecito (1949-51, 1962)

Gross, Robert E. residence, Sandyland Cove, Carpinteria

Tower, Lockwood, Montecito (alterations, 1949, 1962)

Westen, Henrik residence, Montecito (alterations & additions, 1949-50, 1955-57, 1959)

McMillan, P. Dana beach house, Sandyland Cove, Carpinteria (cabana designed with Lockwood De Forest, 1950)

1950
Bill, S.R., beach cottage, Sandyland Cove, Carpinteria
Black, G. Palmer and Louise residence, Montecito (1950-51; 1954)

Hershey, A.L. & The Hershey Beverage Co., refreshment stand, Santa Barbara ?

Proj.: Landon, E. Laird residence, La Jolla

Mazet, Robert residence, Montecito

McRae, Mrs. Floyd W. (Eleanor) residence, Montecito (alterations)

Nelson, Lawrence M. office, Santa Barbara

Sheets, Harold F. residence, Montecito (alterations and additions)

Witter, Guy residence, Sandyland Cove, Carpinteria (additions)

1951
Clifford, George residence, Hope Ranch, (1951-52)

Colman, Ronald residence, Montecito (alterations and additions, 1951-58)

Ducommun, Charles residence, Los Angeles

Hamilton, John B. residence, Montecito

Proj.: Hollister, J.J., Rancho Boleta, Gaviota (housing for ranch help, 1951-52)

Hollister, J.J. residence, Santa Barbara (alterations & additions)

Morf, Howard residence, Montecito (alterations)

Nugent, Daniel residence, Montecito, (alterations, 1951-52)

Peck, Aldrick R. residence, Sandyland Cove, Carpinteria (Alterations & additions, 1951, 1957-58, 1959, 1961)

Wynne, Austin and Watling, Mrs. John residence, Montecito (alterations)

1952
Griffith, Eleanor residence, Montecito (alterations)

Ludington, Wright residence, Montecito (alterations)

McNaughten, Malcolm residence, Montecito (alterations and additions)

Morton, Sterling residence, Montecito (alterations)

1953
Bodman, Harold C. residence, Montecito (additions) (1953, 1957)

Fleming, Wallace F. residence, Montecito

Proj.: Hayes, Mrs. James H. residence, Montecito

Kelleher, Mrs. M. Landreth residence, Montecito

Morse, John Boit residence, Montecito (1953-54)

Nagle, Frank residence, Montecito (alterations & additions, 1953-54, 1955)

Rosenthal, Maurice residence, Santa Barbara (alterations & additions, 1953-54, 1972)

Proj.: Wollman, John residence, Somis

1954
Bacon, G. Norman residence, Hope Ranch (alterations & addition of a guest house, 1954-56)

Proj.: Bear, Mrs. Donald residence, Montecito

Davis, Mrs. George Merrill (Elsie) residence, Santa Barbara

Knowles, Joseph residence, Santa Barbara (alteration & additions, 1954-55)

Miramar Hotel, Montecito (alterations & additions, (1954-55)

Proj.:Oakley, Alfred A. residence, Santa Barbara

Plous, Harold residence, Santa Barbara (1954-55)

Vedanta Temple, for the Vedanta Society of Southern California, Montecito (1954-56); gatehouse (1958-59; 1963); lanterns (1960); carport (1960); Vedanta Pavilion (1960, 1964-65)

1955
Ames, Richard McCurdy cottage residence,Santa Barbara (1955-58)

Proj.: Crockett, Mrs. Charis residence & guest cottage, Montecito

Kiler, E. Leslie residence, Santa Barbara

Lobero Theater (original building by George Washington Smith), Santa Barbara (alterations and additions, 1955-57, 1960, 1963)

San Ysidro Ranch, Montecito (alterations)

Steuard, Ralph residence, Ventura (additions)

Thornburgh, Byron residence, Sandyland Cove, Carptinteria (1955, 1957)

1956
Donohue, Daniel J. residence, "Villa San Giuseppe," Los Angeles (garden, 1956-1966; studio building, 1967)

Packard Adobe, Santa Barbara (alterations)
Pedotti, A.C. residence, Santa Barbara (alterations & additions)

Smith, Austin C. residence, Fernald Point, Montecito (1956-59)

Wiedemann, Edna A. residence, Montecito

1957
Ludington, Wright S. "Hesperides," Montecito (1957-59; garden pavilion, 1962))

Colville, Frances residence, Isla Vista, Goleta

Erdman, C. Pardee residence, Montecito (1957-59)

Proj.: Heimlich, Albert C. residence, Hope Ranch

Montecito County Water District, Filter Plant building, Montecito (alterations)

Proj.: Wagg, Kenneth residence, Montecito

Wilkie, L.A. residence, Montecito (alterations & additions)

1958
McCormick, A. H. residence, Montecito (alterations & additions, 1958-59, 1963)

1959
Harris, Everett L. residence, Montecito (alterations & additions)

Hopkins, Prynce residence, Santa Barbara (alterations & additions, 1959-62, 1969

Joyce, William H. residence, Montecito (alterations & additions, 1959, 1964)

Kelland, Thomas gates, Fernald Point (1959-60)

Kellehed, M.L. residence, Montecito (alterations & additions)

Mallory, Margaret Residence, Montecito (alteration & additions to servants' quarters)

McCormick, Alister H. residence, Montecito (alterations & additions)

Schaffner, Joseph H. residence, Santa Barbara (alterations & additions, 1959, 1961-63)

Proj.: Ruble, A.C. resort complex La Paz, Baja California, Mexico (date unknown)

1960
Hutton, Curtis W. residence, Montecito

Proj.: Jones, John F. residence, Montecito

Nagel, Peter residence (original residence by George Washington Smith), Montecito (alterations, & additions, 1961-62)

1961
Berkey, Peter III residence, Carpinteria

Galvin, John residence, Rancho San Fernando Rey, Santa Ynez Valley

Griffith, Mrs. Dorothy M. residence, Santa Barbara (alterations & additions)

Hutchins, Robert M. residence, Montecito (alterations & additions, 1961-63)

Kellogg, Mrs. Donald (Irma) residence, "Historic Lemon House," Fithian Ranch, Carpinteria (alterations & additions, 1961-62)

Tiers, Alexander residence, Sandyland Cove, Carpinteria (alterations & additions, 1961-62)

1962
Eisberg, Robert residence, Santa Barbara

Proj.: Frankley, L. W. residence, Mesa Vista Ranch, nr. Carpinteria

Proj.: Frawley, Patrick J. residence, Montecito ?

Santa Barbara Botanic Garden, Santa Barbara (alterations & additions to the Library; research wing, 1962-63)

Schleifer, S.B. residence, Santa Barbara (alterations & additions)

Swimmer, H. Frank residence, Santa Barbara (additions)

Westen, Henrik & Kay Building, Santa Barbara (alterations, 1962-63)

1963
Durney, Ruth residence, Santa Barbara (alterations)

El Paseo Arcade Shops, Suski Building Santa Barbara (alteration & additions to El Paseo, exterior facade of the Suski Building; Suski Building, Victor Gruem Assoc., LMR consulting Architect, 1963-1966)

McCormick, Alister H. garden, Rancho Santa Fe

Murray, Stuart S. residence, Montecito (alterations & additions)

Silva, M.A. residence, Montecito (alterations)

1964
Burden, Shirley C. residence, Montecito (alterations & additions, 1964-68, 1973-74)

Forbes, Wilson residence, Montecito (additions)

Fuller, Alvan T. residence, Montecito (additions)

Paul, Winston residence, (formerly Parrott Residence) Fernald Point, Montecito (alterations, addition of swimming pool, 1979)

1965
Proj.: St. Andrew's Episcopal Church , Ojai (alterations & additions, development plan)

1966-1967
Proj.: Jessen, R.H. residence, Carpinteria (alterations & additions)

Watson, Earnest C. residence, Montecito (alterations & additions)

1968
Gooding, Eleanor residence, Santa Paula (alterations & additions, 1968-69)

Herrmann, Eva residence (Vedanta Society of So. California), Montecito

Westen, Henrik residence, Montecito (alterations, 1968-69)

1969
Proj.: Wilson, Page residence, Montecito (alterations)

1970
Donohue, Daniel J. residence, Montecito (formerly Kirk Johnson residence, "Sotto Il Monte, designed by George Washington Smith), Montecito (alterations, 1970-71)

1971
Ordas, Ray residence, Santa Barbara (alterations)

1972
Nash, Roderick residence, Montecito

Proj.:Richardson, Mrs. Jules V. residence, Montecito

1973
Proj.: Becktel, Elizabeth Hay residence, Montecito

Ludington, Wright S. residence, "October Hill," Montecito

1974
Bradley, William residence & barn, Santa Ynez (1974-75)

1975
Proj.: Echols, David residence, Montecito

Proj.: Eckis, Rollin residence, Laguna Beach

Horton, William C. residence, Montecito (additions, not dated, c. 1975)

Loebl, James residence, Ojai (additions, 1975-76)

Proj.: Ryan, Terrence & Stache, Jayne duplex Santa Barbara

1976
Proj.: Baker, Ten Broeck residence, Casitas Pass, Ventura County

Bourlon, Francois residence (formerly Canby-Cunningham designed by George Washington Smith), Montecito (alterations)

Cronshaw, James residence, Santa Barbara (alterations & additions)

Proj.: De L'Arbre, Bertie studio, Santa Barbara (addition)

Kearny, Philip residence, Montecito (additions)

McMahon, Patrick residence, Montecito (additions)

1977
Brand, Ms. residence, (Lindley-Chancellor residence designed by George Washington Smith), Montecito (alterations)

Dibblee, Thomas W. residence, Santa Barbara (alterations & additions)

Proj.: Haskell, Eldon residence, Santa Barbara County

Proj.: Jaccarino, Vincent studio, Santa Barbara (addition)

Lawson, Robert residence, Santa Barbara (alterations)

Louis, Jean residence, Montecito (additions)

Rancho San Julian Dairy onverted to residence, near Lompoc

Shannon, William W. shop & guest barn, Happy Canyon, Santa Ynez

Shorrock, Hallam C. residence, Goleta (additions, 1977-80)

Wallop, John residence, Montecito (additions, 1977-78)

Woodhouse, Charles D. residence, Santa Barbara (alterations & additions)

1978
Antrim, Jack C. residence, Goleta, (1978-80)

Kirkpatrick, Phil residence Santa Barbara (carport addition)

Knapp, Mrs. Gladys residence, Montecito (additions)

1979
Proj.: St. Clair, Michael J. residence, Montecito (alterations)

1980
Ashley, Dennis residence, Santa Barbara (additions)

Dahlen, Gregory A. residence, Hope Ranch (terrace addition)

BIBLIOGRAPHY

Notes, letters, daily calendars and other records of Lutah Maria Riggs are located in the Architectural Drawing Collection, University Art Museum, University of California Santa Barbara. Also in the ADC are a number of taped interviews made in the late 1970s, early 1980s. Participants in these interview were Katherine McMahon, Andy Neumann, William Wittausch, Isabelle Greene, and others. Other records relating to LMR are at the Library of the Santa Barbara Historical Society, The Library of the History Committee, Montecito Association, and Special Collections, the Library, University of California Santa Barbara.

"Winner of News Prize Is Doing Well at School." *Santa Barbara Daily News*, May 20, 1918: Sec 2, 7.

Meany, Philip J., "Winners of the Small Brick House Competition," *Pacific Coast Architect*, 25 (January 1924): 6–17.

"Winning Designs in Brick Home Competition," *Architect and Engineer*, 77 (January 1924): 73–80.

Stow-Fithian, Anne, "The Home of Miss Lutah Riggs, Montecito, California," *Home and Field*, 40 (September 1930): 22.

"California Sunlight Pervades a Little House," *Home and Field*, 41 (January 1931): 33–35, 78.

" 'Clavelitos', The Home of Lutah Maria Riggs, Architect, in Santa Barbara," *California Arts and Architecture*, 40 (July 1931): 28 29.

Phillips, Lily Ann, "A Little Paint Helps Create a Big Impression," *Western Paint Review* 17 (October 1931): 6–8.

Hall, Margaret, "Under the Pebble Beach Cypress," *Town and Country*, 87 (October 15, 1932): 29–33.

"Kitchen in House at Santa Barbara, California," *American Architect*, 147 (September 1935): 45–47.

"Estate of Mr. and Mrs. Allen Breed Walker," *Country Life*, 70 (July 1936): 58–60.

"House for Allen Breed Walker, Montecito, Ca," *Architectural Forum*, 67 (July, 1937): 34–35.

Thompson, Betty, "Small Santa Barbara Homes," *California Arts and Architecture*, 55, (February 1939): 18–20.

Lutah Maria Riggs, "Mediterranean Sources Varied," *Santa Barbara News-Press*, (March 3, 1940): Pt. 3, 17.

Lutah Maria Riggs, "Beautiful Gillespie Estate Fine Example of Mediterranean Type," *Santa Barbara News-Press* (March 17, 1940): Pt. 3, 18.

"For a Family of Two—With Guests," *Sunset*, 97 (September 1946): 24–27.

"Lobero's Place Here Unique," *Santa Barbara News-Press*, January 8, 1949):

"Santa Barbara, Project for a House, Lutah Maria Riggs, Arvin Shaw III, & Oscar Niemeyer, Architects," *Arts and Architecture*, 66 (March 1949): 26–29.

"A House that Kept its Sense of Tradition," *Sunset*, 103 (August 1949): 28–29.

"Gross Beach House, Sandy Land Cove," *Sunset*, 104 (May 1950): Cover, 36–37.

"Simplicity and Livability Stressed in Beach Home of Mr. & Mrs. Robert Gross," *Santa Barbara News-Press* (May 21, 1950): Sec. D, 3.

"Bathroom Planning Ideas," *Sunset* , 106 (June 1951): 56.

"Weekend ranch house," *Sunset*, 107 (August 1951): 38–39.

"A Vacation Home, Simple, Modern, Open to the Sun and Blending into the Sloping Landscape," *Santa Barbara News-Press* (August 5, 1951): Sec. D, 2

Linderman, Verne, "Lutah Riggs, Santa Barbara's Only Licensed Woman Architect, Helped Create the Golden Era—the Era of Spanish Revival," Santa Barbara News-Press (September 9, 1951): Sec. A, 5.

"Is This the Number One Shortcoming of the One-Story Western Home?" *Sunset*, 108 (June 1952): 48.

"Designed into this Country House . . . Comfort in Its Looks and Living, [Beach Cooke House, Montecito]," *Sunset*, 109 (July 1952): 52–53.

"Glass Tent, a Santa Barbara House," *House and Home*, 2 (September 1952): 114–119.

"Magazine Features Montecito Home," *Santa Barbara News-Press* (Aug. 11, 1952): Sec. B,1.

"Sun and Severity," *Time*, 60 (August 11, 1952): 49–52.

"A Car Port Is Often All You Need (Johnson)," *Sunset*, 110 (January 1953): 34.

"Architect Wright Being Invited," *Santa Barbara News-Press* (Jan. 19, 1953): Sec. B, 2.

"California Doctor's Office," *Architectural Record*, 113

(May 1953): 184.

"Dressing Room and Bath," *House Beautiful*, 97 (August 1954): 54–55.

"Living with Antiques," *Antiques* 64 (November 1953): 388.

Linderman, Verne, "Apartment Uses Space Ingeniously," *Santa Barbara News*-Press (March 13, 1955): Sec. B, 5.

"Have You Discovered the New Plastics Building Panels?," *House Beautiful*, 97 (July 1955): 57–69, 127.

Barry, Joseph A., "An Interview with the People Who Live in This House," *House Beautiful*, 97 (October 1955): 182–189, 248.

Linderman, Verne. "A Spanish Town House: Pedottis Develop Picturesque Studio Into Part-Time Residence," *Santa Barbara News-Press* (August 18, 1957): Sec. D, 8.

"In Santa Barbara, an unusual remodel . . . With the quiet charm of an old Spanish ranch house. . . ," *Sunset* 119 (September 1957): 54–57.

Aloi, Roberto. *Camini D'Oggi*. (Milan: Ulrico Hoepli, 1957): 156.

"E. Leslie Kiler House," *Book of Homes*, 14 (1958): 39–41.

"Leisurely Charm Keynotes Heimlichs Contemporary Home in Hope Ranch," *Santa Barbara News-Press* (April 5, 1959): Sec. C, 14.

"This Inner-Court House Used to Be Two Separate Buildings," *House Beautiful*, 101 (November 1959): 296–299.

Linderman, Verne, "8 Outside Doors Featured in Surfside Home of Retired Business Executive," *Santa Barbara News-Press* (December 27, 1959): Sec. C, 13.

Paulding, Litti, "Institute of Architects Will Honor Lutah Riggs," *Santa Barbara News-Press* (February 28, 1960): Sec. A, 11, 16.

"New Fellows of The American Institute of Architects," *Journal of the American Institute of Architects*, 33 (June 1960): 52–56.

"The Good Cook's Kitchen," *Sunset* 125 (November 1960): 86–99.

Besinger, Curtis, "How to Take Full Advantage of Your Site," *House Beautiful*, (May 1961): 102–109, 160, 163 & 164.

Linderman. Verne. "Wood Interior Brings Warmth to House by the Sea," *Santa Barbara News-Press* (May 14, 1961): Sec. A, 22.

"Names," *Architectural & Engineering News* (June 1962): 73.

"Pasadenan's Beach Home Is More Than Summer Place," *Santa Barbara News-Press* (August 19, 1962): Sec. C, 19.

Gebhard, David. "The Governor's Mansion Competition," *Art Forum* 1 (1962): 34–35.

"Botanic Garden Event: Research Facility Due Sunday," *Santa Barbara News-Press* (October 25, 1962): Sec. C, 3.

Blair, Kim. "Lutah Riggs—A Designing Woman," *Los Angeles Times* (October 17, 1966): Sec. 4, 1 & 13.

Faulkner, Maurice. "Times Woman of the Year: Lutah Maria Riggs Honored," *Los Angeles Times* (December 13, 1966): Sec. B, 1.

Vils, Ursula. "Nine Receive Award as Times Women of the Year: Honored for Distinguished Service to Community in Various Fields," *Los Angeles Times* (December 13, 1966): Sec. 2, 3.

"Capsule Reports on 1966 Award Winners, Achievements," *Los Angeles Times* (December 13, 1966): Sec. 4, 1, 8 & 9.

Seidenbaum, Art. "Lutah Riggs Lines Up the Future," *Los Angeles Times* (January 4, 1967): Sec. 5, 1 & 6.

Linderman, Verne. "Lutah Maria Riggs: Making an Impact as an Architect," *Santa Barbara News-Press* (Feb. 2, 1975): Sec. D, 2.

Rochlin, Harriet. "A Distinguished Generation of Women Architects in California," *Journal of the American Institute of Architects*, 66: (August 1977): 38–42.

Gebhard, David, & Nevins, Deborah. *200 Years of American Architectural Drawing*. (New York: Whitney Library of Design, 1977): 228–229.

Paine, Jocelyn. "Exhibit Recognizes Women's Largely Obscured Architectural Contributions," *Los Angeles Times* (April 30, 1978): Sec. 7, 20, 22–23.

Dreyfuss, John. "Women's Work in Architecture," *Los Angeles Times* (May 18, 1978): Sec. 4, 1, 8–9.

Jackson, Beverley. "Preservation Project," *Santa Barbara News-Press* (September 10, 1978): Sec. E, 1.

McCoy, Esther, "A Walk With Lutah Riggs," *LA Architect* 5 (July 1979): 3.

"Week of Events Planned by Architects," *Santa Barbara News-Press* (September 16, 1979): Sec. F, 3.

Ames, Richard. "Two Recent Shows Qualify Simply as Memorabilia," *Santa Barbara News-Press* (September 22, 1979): Sec. C, 17.

Nevins, Deborah, & Stern, Robert A.M. *The Architect's Eye*. (New York: Pantheon Books, 1979): 120–121.

Andree, Herb, & Young, Noel; Photographs by Wayne McCall. (2nd Edition edited & designed by Bob Easton and Wayne McCall). *Santa Barbara Architecture.* (Capra Press, 1980): 149, 194–195, 216, 270–272 & 287.

Weaver, Judy, "Grande Dame of Design Still Thrives," *Santa Barbara News-Press* (November 9, 1981): Sec. B, 1–2.

"Lutah Maria Riggs Dies at 87; noted Santa Barbara Architect," *Santa Barbara News-Press* (March 9, 1984): Sec. B, 3.

"Riggs Memorial," *Santa Barbara News-Press* (March 18, 1984): Sec. E, 21.

Folkart, Burt A. "Lutah Maria Riggs, Celebrated Santa Barbara Architect, Dies," *Los Angeles Times* (March 21, 1984): Sec. PII, 4.

Gebhard, David. "Obituary [of Lutah Maria Riggs]," *Architecture* 73 (May 1984): 378.

"Obituary [Lutah Maria Riggs]," *Progressive Architecture,* 65 (May 1984): 29.

Rouse, Stella Haverland. "Lutah Maria Riggs," *Noticias,* 30 (Summer 1984): 36–39.

"Lutah M. Riggs Exhibit on Display February 1," *Montecito Life* (January 17, 1985): 7.

Churchill, Maria. "Remembering Lutah Riggs—A Remarkable Woman Who Succeeded in a Man's World," *Montecito Life* (May 22, 1986): 6.

Crowder, Joan. "Vedanta: Serenity Seekers," *Santa Barbara News-Press* (March 6, 1988): Sec. D, 1 & 10.

Ouwehand, Terre. "Lutah Maria Riggs: Architect," *Santa Barbara Magazine,* 16 (Jan/Feb 1990): 36–41, 53 & 62

INDEX